MISSIONARY TONGUES REVISITED

More than an Evidence:

Recapturing Luke's
Missional Perspective on
Speaking in Tongues

Denzil R. Miller
© 2014

Unless otherwise noted Scripture quotations are from *The Holy Bible, English Standard Version* (ESV®), copyright © 2001 by Crossway, a publishing ministry of Good News Publishers. Used by permission. All rights reserved.

Miller, Denzil R., 1946–
Missionary Tongues Revisited: More Than an Evidence: Recapturing Luke's Missional Perspective on Speaking in Tongues / Denzil R. Miller

1. Biblical Studies–Acts. 2. Theology. 3. Pentecostal.
4. Holy Spirit. 5. Missions. 6. Tongues–Glossolalia

ISBN 978-0-9911332-6-0

Printed in the United States of America
PneumaLife Publications, Springfield, MO, USA
2014

CONTENTS

PREFACE

During the past two decades as director of the Acts in Africa Initiative (AIA)[1] it has been my privilege to travel throughout Africa conducting pastors' conferences, ministering in local churches, and teaching in theological seminaries. During these years, I, along with my AIA team members, have conducted national Holy Spirit conferences (we call them Acts 1:8 Conferences) in 32 countries in sub-Sahara Africa and the Indian Ocean Basin. In these conferences we have seen in attendance as few as 30 and as many as 13,000 pastors. One of the highlights of my ministry in Africa has been the privilege of praying with, and watching God fill, thousands of believers with the Holy Spirit accompanied by speaking in tongues just as described in the New Testament book of Acts.

In spite of these wonderful experiences, I have observed what appears to me to be a disturbing trend in the Pentecostal church in Africa.[2] Across the continent there is a growing

---

[1] The Acts in Africa Initiative is a missionary ministry working under the auspices of the Africa Assemblies of God Alliance (AAGA) and the U.S. Assemblies of God World Missions–Africa Office (AGWM-Africa). Its mission is to help mobilize the Africa Assemblies of God for Spirit-empowered mission (cf. www.ActsinAfrica.org and www.DecadeofPentecost.org).

[2] I have observed this same trend in America, and I believe it to be a worldwide phenomenon in Pentecostalism.

tendency on the part of pastors to neglect the Pentecostal experience in their churches. Pentecostal pastors who once preached often on the baptism in the Holy Spirit and prayed with their members to be filled have moved onto other more appealing topics, such as the temporal blessings of wealth and prosperity. Even when these pastors do occasionally preach on the subject of Spirit baptism, they couch the experience more in the contemporary context of personal blessing rather than in the missional context so clearly described in the book of Acts.

Along with this neglect of the experience, there has been an accompanying loss of understanding of its true nature and purpose. I am convinced that this failure of Pentecostal ministers to address the subject in any compelling way has been fueled, at least in part, by a shallow and misdirected understanding of the Pentecostal experience itself—along with a consequent misunderstanding of the missional nature of its accompanying sign, speaking in tongues.

Although in other works I have written on the subject of speaking in tongues,[3] I have not dealt adequately with the missional nature of the practice, nor have I found any other work that significantly addresses the subject. In this book I hope to begin to remedy that deficiency. In doing this, I will draw on my years of personal study on the subject, from my

---

[3] I have discussed the subject of speaking in tongues in two of my earlier books, *In Step with the Spirit*, Chapter 3, "The Gateway to Life in the Spirit" (31-48), Chapter 8, "Speaking in Tongues: What Good is It?" (103-116), and Chapter 5, "Intercessory Prayer in the Spirit" (143-152); and in *Empowered for Global Mission: A Missionary Look at the Book of Acts,* Chapter 14, "Evidential Tongues" (319-338).

discussions with fellow pastors and scholars, from my practical experience in the field, and hopefully from the Spirit Himself.

I gratefully acknowledge my indebtedness to my mentors and colleagues, both African and American, who have contributed to my understanding of the subject. I am especially indebted to the insights I have received from my many classroom discussions with students whom I have taught and mentored at All Nations Theological Seminary in Lilongwe, Malawi; East Africa Graduate Studies Center in Nairobi, Kenya; and Pan-Africa Theological Seminary, in Lome, Togo, and Nairobi, Kenya.

I commend this work to you for your examination, believing that the insights contained herein could have a dramatic impact on our mutual understanding of the missional purpose and nature of speaking in tongues as presented by Luke in the book of Acts. I further hope that this fresh understanding of tongues will help to spark a new era of preaching and teaching on the subject resulting in millions of new believers being baptized in the Holy Spirit accompanied by the normative missional sign of speaking in tongues as the Spirit enables, and resulting in greater Spirit-empowered witness at home and to the ends of the earth (Acts 1:8).

Preface

INTRODUCTION

From its beginnings the practice of speaking in tongues has been a distinctive hallmark of the modern Pentecostal movement. In recent years, however, a noticeable "experiential drift" has occurred in Pentecostal circles. Statistical reports reveal an ever-declining percentage of members of Pentecostal churches who claim to have been baptized in the Holy Spirit accompanied by Spirit-inspired speaking in tongues as described in the New Testament book of Acts.[4] While many within the movement view this trend with alarm, others are seemingly unmoved by the development.

Throughout the movement's history the practice of speaking in tongues has paradoxically served to both attract people to and repel them from Pentecostal churches. Some see the practice as an evidence of God's hand on the movement, an indication that the God of Scripture is alive and actively at work among His people. Others see tongues as a means by

---

[4] In *Gift and Giver: The Holy Spirit for Today,* Craig S. Keener states, "Statistics suggest that a large percentage of Pentecostals do not speak in tongues! (Some argue that over half of Pentecostals)" (Grand Rapids, MI: Baker Academic, 2001, 181). He further cites Henry Lederle who states that only 35% of all Pentecostals have ever spoken in tongues ("Evidence and Movement," in *Initial Evidence,* ed. Gary B. McGee (Peabody, MS: Hendrickson, 1991, 136).

which God is unifying His church across historic denomina-
tional, racial, and socioeconomic divides, "allow[ing] the
poor, uneducated, and illiterate among the people of God to
have an equal voice with the educated and literate."[5] Conversely, others perceive the practice as aberrant and a barrier
to evangelical unity.[6]

In more recent years some Pentecostals have, for various
reasons, sought to distance themselves from the practice. More
"seeker-sensitive" pastors, drawing inspiration from prominent, non-Pentecostal church leaders, and not wanting to
offend visitors to their churches, have opted to dismiss the
practice all together, or at least to limit its practice to the
backrooms of the church. Others, fearing the misuse of the
gift, have banned its public practice entirely, especially from
their "pre-evangelistic" Sunday morning services. Still others,
having observed the questionable lives of some who speak in
tongues, as well as the unrestrained misuse of the gift in
certain contexts, have determined that the practice has little
contemporary value, and have chosen not to incorporate it into
their own personal spiritual lives or ministries. Pentecostal
educator, Robert Crosby, observes that, while the largest

---

[5] Frank Macchia, "The Struggle for Global Witness: Shifting
Paradigms in Pentecostal Theology," in *The Globalization of
Pentecostalism,* ed. Murray W. Dempster, et al. (Irvine, CA:
Regnum Books, 1999), 18.

[6] Craig Keener quotes D. A Carson in *Showing the Spirit*
(Grand Rapids, MI: Baker Book House, 1987, 50) as saying, "If
the Pentecostal movement would firmly renounce, on biblical
grounds, not the gift of tongues, but the idea that tongues consti-
tute a sign of special blessing, a very substantial part of the wall
between charismatics and noncharismatics would come crashing
down" (Gift and Giver, 174).

Pentecostal organization in the world, the Assemblies of God, considers tongues to be the "initial physical evidence" of the baptism in the Holy Spirit, and in its official statement calls on believers to "earnestly seek" to be filled with the Spirit, oddly, it "seems that this hallmark phenomenon over the past decade has on many fronts been de-emphasized, displaced, and in some cases, even placed on hold within churches that still consider themselves 'Pentecostal.'"[7] These and other factors have contributed to the considerable experiential drift that has taken place in many Pentecostal churches.

Along with this experiential drift, there has been a concomitant theological drift within the movement concerning the Classical Pentecostal doctrines of subsequence and evidential tongues.[8] Several years ago a ministerial colleague of mine quipped, "All year long I'm confused about what I believe on the subject; however, when it comes time for me to renew my ministerial credentials, *I know exactly what I believe!*" While we all laughed at his jest, still, it left me with an uneasy feeling in my gut. I wondered, is there a serious underlying spiritual reality cloaked in this brother's humorous

---

[7] Robert Crosby, "The Pentecostal Paradox: As the Global Chorus Grows, American Tongues Fall Silent," Patheos.com: http://www.patheos.com/Resources/Additional-Resources/ Pentecostal-Paradox-Robert-Crosby-01-27-2012.html (accessed February 19, 2014).

[8] The term *subsequence* refers to the Pentecostal teaching that the baptism in the Holy Spirit is an experience separate from and subsequent to (if not always experientially, at least logically and theologically) the new birth. The term *evidential tongues* refers to the Classical Pentecostal doctrine that everyone who is baptized in the Holy Spirit will speak in other tongues as did the first disciples on the Day of Pentecost (Acts 2:4; cf. 10:46; 19:6).

remark? This incident exemplifies the ambiguity felt by many today who associate themselves with Pentecostal churches. While most have some level of awareness concerning the experience, they are nevertheless unable to clearly articulate its nature, meaning, or purpose. As a result, many have little desire to experience it in their own lives. A core theological tenet that once shaped the Pentecostal psyche is now held only tentatively by a majority of the movement's adherents. Until we clearly understand the true nature and purpose of the experience that speaking in tongues signifies—that is, Spirit baptism as presented by Luke in the book of Acts—we will never have a clear understanding of its accompanying phenomenon, Spirit-enabled speaking in tongues.

This book is my effort to shed light on this reality. In its pages I will endeavor to bring these two critical biblical understandings together, that is, an understanding of the gift of the Holy Spirit itself, along with a clearer understanding of the speaking in tongues which Luke so closely associates with the gift. I hope to demonstrate how Luke symbiotically links these two deeply spiritual experiences into a common missiological whole. In doing this, I will attempt to unwrap his missional understanding of speaking in tongues as presented in his two-part history of Christian beginnings, Luke-Acts, and as intuitively grasped by early twentieth-century Pentecostals. I hope to at least begin to lay a biblical foundation concerning Luke's unique missional presentation of both the experience of Spirit baptism itself and of the sign that accompanies it.

In Chapter 1, I discuss early Pentecostalism's bold experiment with xenolalic "missionary tongues." In doing this I note the strong missional connections these first-generation Pentecostals made between the experience of Spirit baptism, its "Bible sign" (as they called it) of speaking in tongues, and the evangelization of the nations. Unfortunately, however, as Pentecostals distanced themselves from this early xenolalic teaching on tongues, they concurrently lost the connection between speaking in tongues and missionary advance of the church. Since that time, the predominant Pentecostal understanding of speaking in tongues has steadily shifted away from Luke's missional perspective as presented in Acts to Paul's congregational perspective as presented in his epistles. This lack of clear biblical understanding concerning tongues as a missional enablement has, in my opinion, mitigated the impact of the experience on the lives of believers and in the missionary advance of the church.

In Chapter 2, "Recapturing a Missional View of Tongues," I discuss how the emergence of new interpretative approaches has enabled contemporary Pentecostal scholars to more forcefully articulate Luke's missional and prophetic view of Spirit baptism. Unfortunately, Pentecostal scholars have not adequately applied these new approaches to the issue of speaking in tongues. I call on Pentecostals to revisit and recapture Luke's missional view of speaking in tongues.

In the next four chapters I investigate Luke's missional view of tongues as portrayed in the book of Acts, noting how the Classical Pentecostal doctrine of "initial physical evidence," while true in itself, is an incomplete understanding of Luke's missional presentation of tongues. In his missionary history of the beginnings of the church Luke presents tongues in at least four distinct, yet interrelated, ways. First, in Chapter 3 I discuss how Luke presents tongues as *confirmatory evidence,* indicating that one has indeed been baptized in the

Holy Spirit as promised by Jesus and modeled by believers in the book of Acts (compare 1:4-5; 10:46-47; and 11:15-16). Then, in Chapter 4 I discuss how Luke further presents tongues as a *missional sign.* For him speaking in tongues is more than an evidence, it is a sign that speaks to the deeper meaning and purpose of the experience. It signifies that Spirit baptism is a prophetic enablement to proclaim the gospel to the nations in the power of the Holy Spirit (1:8; 2:5-11, 16-21).

Next, in Chapter 5 I discuss how Luke further presents speaking in tongues as a *prophetic release,* noting how in Acts he always couples speaking in tongues with Spirit-inspired speech in the vernacular (cf. 2:4 with 14ff; 10:47; 19:6). In doing this, he wants his readers to see how the disciples' speaking in tongues effects a powerful inner release in their hearts enabling them speak prophetically in the common language. He thus presents tongues, not as an end in them-selves, but as means to a greater end, that is, Spirit-inspired proclamation of the gospel to the lost. Finally, in Chapter 6 I suggest that in Acts Luke presents tongues as an *enabling element.* In this way he sees tongues, not merely as a cosmetic postscript to Spirit baptism, but as part and parcel of the empowering experience. This is especially evident when Luke's missional perspective on tongues as presented in Acts is combined with Paul's exhortation in 1 Corinthians 14:4 that "the one who speaks in a tongue builds up himself." I con-clude in Chapter 7 with an appeal to Pentecostals to (re)discover Luke's compelling missional view of speaking in tongues.

It preparation for our theological inquiry it will be helpful if we pause to briefly review how the Classical Pentecostal understanding of speaking in tongues has shifted during the one-hundred years since the movement began and how that shift has significantly impacted the way speaking in tongues is taught and experienced in the Pentecostal church today. This we will do in Chapter 1.

INTRODUCTION

– CHAPTER 1 –

EARLY PENTECOSTALISM'S GRAND EXPERIMENT WITH "MISSIONARY TONGUES"

Unlike many contemporary Pentecostals, first-generation Pentecostals had little ambivalence concerning the experience of Spirit baptism. They truly believed that they had received the Latter Rain gift of the Holy Spirit promised by the prophet Joel and experienced by the apostles and believers in the New Testament church.[9] They were further convinced that they had received this experience in the same manner as those first century disciples, with the "Bible evidence" of speaking in

---

[9] The message of the "Latter Rain" was a common theme among early Pentecostals. They widely believed that the outpouring of the Spirit they were experiencing was a fulfillment of Joel's ancient promise that in the final days of time God would abundantly pour out His Spirit as a "latter rain" bringing in a worldwide harvest of souls just before the coming of Christ (cf., Joel 2:23-28; James 5:7-8). For example, the headline of the second edition of *The Apostolic Faith* newspaper published by the Azusa Street Mission boldly declared, "The Pentecostal Baptism Restored: The Promised Latter Rain Now Being Poured out on God's Humble People" (Los Angeles: October, 1906).

other tongues as the Spirit gave them utterance. Although, early on, there was a handful of detractors to the idea of normative tongues, by the end of the revival's first decade the issue was largely settled.[10] This certainty concerning the necessity of every believer being baptized in the Spirit accompanied by speaking in tongues as the Spirit gave utterance served to align the movement, and its "initial physical evidence" doctrinal formation became a major contributor to its cohesion and phenomenal expansion. I will discuss this idea more in Chapter 3, "Tongues as a Confirmatory Evidence."

"Missionary Tongues" Embraced

An important development in early Pentecostalism was the emergence of the concept of "missionary tongues." Although the notion was soon to be discarded, the teaching was embraced by early leaders of the movement, including such notables as Charles F. Parham and William J. Seymour. Because of his teaching concerning the Bible evidence of the baptism in the Holy Spirit, and his application of those teachings at the Bethel Bible School in Topeka, Kansas, in late 1900 and early 1901, Parham is widely recognized as the "theological father" of the modern Pentecostal movement.[11] His teachings concerning

---

[10] Gary B. McGee, "Early Pentecostal Hermeneutics: Tongues as Evidence in the Book of Acts," in *Evidential Tongues,* ed. Gary B. McGee (Peabody, MA: Hendrickson Publishers, 1991), 96-118.

[11] Vinson Synan, "The Lasting Legacies of the Azusa Street Revival," http://enrichmentjournal.ag.org/200602/200602_142_legacies.cfm (accessed March 20, 2014); James R. Goff, Jr., *Fields White unto Harvest: Charles F. Parham and the Missionary Origins of Pentecostalism* (Fayetteville: AR: University of Arkansas Press, 1988), 164-165.

speaking in tongues were subsequently embraced and advanced by his protégée, William J. Seymour, spiritual leader of the famed Azusa Street Revival in Los Angeles. Although, following his bitter falling out with Parham in late 1906 Seymour began to qualify his views concerning speaking in tongues, in the early days of the revival he held to and vigorously promoted Parham's teaching.

Each of these men referred to speaking in tongues as the scriptural evidence of one's having been baptized in the Holy Spirit, and viewed them as an eschatological sign heralding the soon coming of Christ. They, however, saw speaking in tongues as much more than this; they saw the practice as a supernatural enablement to preach the gospel in unlearned languages as promised by Jesus in Mark 16:17 and as exemplified by the 120 on the Day of Pentecost (Acts 2:6-11).

This early theological stance was significantly different from that of their Pentecostal successors. Parham and Seymour believed that the Spirit-engendered tongues spoken at Spirit baptism were actual, known foreign languages (sometimes referred to as *xenolalia* or *xenoglossa*) rather than heavenly or spiritual ones (known as *glossolalia*). They believed that the reception of these God-given tongues would eliminate the time consuming need for missionaries to learn foreign languages, and would thus expedite the spread of the gospel to the unreached peoples and places of the world before the approaching end of the age. They further believed that, in order for a person to be truly baptized in the Holy Spirit, he or she must speak in a living human language. Any other "evidence" was deemed as inadequate and, therefore, did not signify a full baptism in the Holy Spirit. As would their successors, they also held that the purpose of Spirit baptism was an "enduement with power for service."[12]

Parham's view concerning speaking in tongues was undoubtedly influenced by the teachings of the so-called "radical evangelicals" of the late nineteenth century. For instance, A. B. Simpson, the revered missionary statesman and founder of the Christian and Missionary Alliance, looked for an outpouring of the Spirit resulting in the restoration of New Testament signs and wonders, including "missionary tongues." These miraculous signs would enable the rapid evangelization of the nations before Jesus' soon coming to establish His thousand-year reign on earth.[13] This idea of missionary tongues was also shared by the famed Cambridge Seven[14] and taught by Frank W. Sanford at his Holy Ghost and Us Bible School in Shiloh, Maine, where Parham spent time before founding his Bethel Bible School in

---

[12] Douglas Jacobsen, *Thinking in the Spirit: Theologies of the Early Pentecostal Movement* (Bloomington, IN: Indiana University Press, 2003), 49.

[13] "All for Jesus: The Revival Legacy of A.B. Simpson," by Gary B. McGee in *Enrichment Journal*, http://enrichmentjournal. ag.org/199903/ 068_tongues.cfm (accessed October 21, 2013).

[14] C.T. Studd, "Trumpet Calls to Britain's Sons," in *The Evangelisation of the World, a Missionary Band: A Record of Consecration, and an Appeal*, 3rd ed., ed. B Broomhall (London: Morgan and Scott, 1889, 53), cited by Gary B. McGee in "Shortcut to Language Preparation? Radical Evangelicals, Missions, and the Gift of Tongues" in *International Journal of Missionary Research* (July 2001, 119).

Topeka, Kansas, in late 1900.[15]

Because of their belief in missionary tongues, Parham and the 34 (or so) students attending his Bethel Bible School in Topeka, Kansas, spent considerable time and energy seeking to discern the language(s) being spoken by individual students who had received the Spirit. Agnes Ozman, the first person to be filled with the Spirit at the school, claimed to have "talked in several languages, and it was clearly manifest when a new dialect was spoken."[16] Some of the languages claimed to have been spoken at Bethel Bible School were Bohemian, Chinese, French, Spanish, Russian, Syrian, Zulu, Swahili, Hindi, and Mandarin.

Parham's belief in missionary tongues was subsequently embraced by Seymour and the other leaders of the Azusa Street Revival in Los Angeles. In the first four editions of *The Apostolic Faith* newspaper published in late 1906, there were no less than 39 explicit reports of xenolalic tongues, with several testifying to have spoken multiple languages. Notably, the speaking in tongues at Azusa Street was more often than not characterized as preaching/proclamation rather than prayer/praise as the movement would later redefine the phenomenon.

For example, the very first edition of *The Apostolic Faith,* the official organ of the Azusa Street Mission, reported, "Many

---

[15] James R. Goff, Jr., "Initial Tongues in the Theology of Charles Fox Parham" in *Evidential Tongues: Historical and Biblical Perspectives on the Pentecostal Doctrine of Spirit Baptism,* ed. Gary B. McGee (Peabody, MA: Hendrickson Publishers, 1991), 63-65.

[16] Stanley Frodsham, *With Signs Following* (Springfield, MO: Gospel Publishing House, 1946).

are speaking in new tongues, and some are on their way to the foreign fields, with the gift of language."[17] Later in the same edition, the editors urged their readers, "Let us lift up Christ to the world in all His fullness, not only in healing and salvation from all sin, but in His power to speak all the languages of the world."[18] In the third edition they triumphantly exulted, "God is solving the missionary problem, sending out new-tongued missionaries on the apostolic faith line, without purse or scrip, and the Lord is going before them preparing the way."[19] These "new tongued missionaries" left the mission convinced that they had been supernaturally equipped to preach the gospel to the nations without the need for language study.

This concept of missionary tongues reveals the strong connection early Pentecostals made between the phenomenon of speaking in tongues and fulfilling the Great Commission of Christ. Douglas Jacobsen notes,

> Parham believed that the sign of tongues was intimately connected with the deeper purpose of the baptism of the Spirit. The ability to speak in other tongues was a special empowerment for end-time service, especially the end-time work of evangelism. Parham said: "Pentecost is given as power to witness." The power of Pentecost was the power to communicate the gospel effectively to others: "the

---

[17] *The Apostolic Faith,* Vol. I, No. 1, September, 1906, Los Angeles.

[18] Ibid.

[19] Ibid., Vol. I, No. 3, November, 1906.

power for witnessing in your own or any language of the world."[20]

Missionary Tongues Abandoned

Eventually, after several disappointing experiences on the foreign field, the practice of missionary tongues was deemed untenable, and Pentecostalism's bold missionary experiment was abandoned. Notwithstanding, the Pentecostal priority on speaking in tongues remained at center stage. The movement's scholars set themselves to reexamining their stance on the nature and purpose of speaking in tongues. This reexamination resulted in, among other things, the emergence of the "initial physical evidence" construct still held by most Classical Pentecostals today. By combining Luke's missional/proclamational perspective of tongues with Paul's spiritual-gift/ heavenly-prayer-language perspective, they developed a more comprehensive understanding of the experience. According to Frank D. Macchia,

> In the decades following the beginnings of pentecostalism, the more Pauline notion of tongues as an in-depth prayer language for self-edification or a congregational gift ... came to dominate the pentecostal understanding of tongues.... glossolalia as a transcendent form of speech or a "heavenly language" came to represent the most common understanding of tongues.[21]

---

[20] Jacobsen, 49.

[21] Frank D. Macchia, "Theology, Pentecostal" in *The New International Dictionary of Pentecostal and Charismatic Movements: Revised and Expanded Edition,* ed. Stanley M. Burgess (Grand Rapids, MI: Zondervan, 2002), 1132.

In his book, *Fire from Heaven,* Harvey Cox describes this shift in emphasis:

> For early pentecostals ... tongue speaking was not just a delightful experience. It had clear theological purpose.... [it] was God's wondrous way of equipping them to make known to every tribe and nation the urgent news that the Last Days were at hand.... The "latter rain" had begun to fall, and the Holy Spirit was pouring out upon the faithful the gifts they would need to make the message known.[22]

Cox continues, "By the end of the decade after the birth of the movement, many followers of the new faith—both black and white—had begun to think of the gift of tongues more in the terms Paul had used in the Epistle to the Romans," that is, as a means of Spirit-enabled intercessory prayer (Rom. 8:26).[23] Thus, speaking in tongues was no longer viewed as an eschatological sign that the last days had come, or as a means of evangelizing the nations. In the words of Cox, "It was understood not primarily as a supernatural tool for world mission but as a ... graceful provision to those who did not have the strength or the fluency to pray with the own words."[24]

---

[22] Harvey Cox, *Fire from Heaven: The Rise of Pentecostal Spirituality and the Reshaping of Religion in the Twenty-first Century* (Cambridge, MA: Da Capo Press, 200), 87.

[23] Ibid.

[24] Ibid.

Luke's Missional View of Tongues Lost

There was a definite downside to this theological re-envisioning concerning the nature and purpose of speaking in tongues. With the abandonment the concept of missionary tongues came a marked diminishing of the movement's corporate consciousness of the missionary nature of the experience of Spirit baptism itself. Over time, Paul's self-edificational view of tongues came to dominate Pentecostal thinking, and Luke's missional view was all but lost, especially in popular teaching and practice.

The emergence of subsequent renewalist movements[25] further affected the way Classical Pentecostals came to view speaking in tongues. The Charismatic Renewal beginning in the 1960's emphasized the Pauline prayer and personal self-edification aspects of speaking in tongues. It was out of this renewal that the terminology of "heavenly prayer language" gained widespread popularity. Two decades later, in true Reformed evangelical fashion, Third Wavers doctrinally subsumed Spirit baptism into the experience of Christian conversion. They opted for what C. Peter Wagner has termed a "low-key acceptance of tongues as one of many NT spiritual gifts that God gives to some and not to others."[26] They came to view

---

[25] "Renewalist" is an umbrella term used by the Pew Form and other researchers to refer to the various Pentecostal/charismatic movements. *Spirit and Power: A 10-Country Survey of Pentecostals* (Washington, D.C.: Pew Research Center, 2007), 12.

[26] C. Peter Wagner, "Third Wave," in *The New International Dictionary of Pentecostal and Charismatic Movements: Revised and Expanded Edition,* ed. Stanley M. Burgess (Grand Rapids, MI: Zondervan, 2002, 1141). In *Acts of the Holy Spirit* Wagner states that most in the Third Wave, which he calls the New Apostolic

tongues, not as a unique and essential accompaniment of the Spirit's empowering work, but merely as one of the *charismata* available only to certain Spirit-filled believers.[27] Both the Charismatic and Third Wave views have significantly affected the way contemporary Classical Pentecostals conceive speaking in tongues and have helped to further obscure the missional nature of the experience as presented by Luke in the book of Acts. I will discuss this idea more later on in this book.

This historical evolution of ideas concerning the nature and purpose of speaking in tongues has unwittingly resulted in the devaluing of the practice in the minds of many contemporary Pentecostals. Since Spirit baptism, along with its accompanying sign of speaking in tongues, are no longer viewed as normative in many Pentecostal circles, they are no longer actively advocated for nor sought after. The subconscious logic is as follows: if the experience is about self-edification and personal blessing, it must therefore be optional, and since I am already

---

Reformation, "regards speaking in tongues a common, but not a necessary, part of Christian life" (74-75).

[27] Wagner, writes, "Although speaking in tongues can be an evidence ... other evidences can be new intimacy with the Father, the joy of the Holy Spirit, falling in the power of God, power to heal the sick and cast out demons, prophecy, a driving passion for winning the lost and many others," (*Acts of the Holy Spirit,* 173). Third Waver, Charles H. Kraft writes, "Though the gift often accompanies the receiving of the Holy Spirit, this is not always the case either in contemporary experience or in the book of Acts.... And according to 1 Cor. 12:30, not everyone needs to receive the gift to be considered valid" ("A Third-wave Perspective on Pentecostal Missions," in *Called and Empowered: Global Empowered: Global Mission in Pentecostal Perspective,* eds. Murray Dempster, et. all, 309).

sufficiently edified and blessed, I choose not to seek the gift. As a result of these and other factors, the early Pentecostal urgency to be empowered by the Spirit and speak in tongues in order to evangelize the nations before the soon coming of Christ has been significantly dampened.

Providentially, however, in recent years there has arisen among Pentecostals a renewed passion to evangelize the un-reached people, peoples, and places of the earth[28] before the soon coming of Christ.[29] Now, as the worldwide Pentecostal church mobilizes to reach these yet-to-be-reached peoples and places, the time is ripe for a bold reexamination and a timely rediscovery of the missional purpose of Spirit baptism as presented by Luke in the book of Acts—along with a rediscovery of his missional presentation of the accompanying sign of speaking in tongues.

To be clear, in this work I am *not* calling for a return to the early Pentecostals' fascination with xenolalic tongues. What I *am* calling for, however, is a rediscovery of the symbiotic missional connection Luke makes between speaking in tongues

---

[28] In His Great Commissions Jesus spoke of reaching *every person* (Mark 16:15: "every creature," KJV), *all peoples* (Matt. 28:19: "all nations") and *every place* (Acts 1:8: "in Jerusalem and in all Judea and Samaria, and to the end of the earth").

[29] For instance, at a recent "Beyond Conference" held in Nairobi, Kenya, on January 7-9, 2014, Assemblies of God (USA) missionary leaders from around the world gathered to discuss how the movement can effectively engage the unreached peoples of the world before the soon coming of Christ.

and the empowering experience they signify. This connection
will become clearer as we proceed through this study.

– CHAPTER 2 –

MORE THAN AN EVIDENCE: RECAPTURING A MISSIONAL VIEW OF TONGUES

Ultimately, one's theology of speaking in tongues must be drawn, not from Pentecostal history, nor from personal experience, but from Scripture. Therefore, in the following chapters we will look to Scripture for answers and insight. The two primary biblical sources for the doctrine and practice of tongues are the writings of Luke in Acts (2:4; 10:46; 19:6) and the writings of Paul in 1 Corinthians (12:10, 28-31; 13:1, 8; 14:1-22; 39), and to a lesser degree in Romans 8:26-28. Pentecostals have also historically appealed to Jesus' mention of speaking in tongues in His Great Commission as it appears in Mark 16:17.

Reconnecting 1:8 and 2:4

Almost universally New Testament scholars cite Acts 1:8 as the "key verse" of the book of Acts. In doing this, they normally point out how the verse serves as an outline, or virtual "table of contents," for the book as follows: (1) the church's witness in Jerusalem (1:1-8:1a); (2) the church's witness in

Judea and Samaria (8:1b-12:25); and (3) the church's witness to the ends of the earth (13:1-28:31).

While this insight is important to one's understanding Acts, it is even more important that the interpreter appreciates how 1:8 serves as more than a mere outline of the book. In a greater measure the verse serves as the interpretative key to one's grasping the core message and guiding theme of the entire work.[30] By quoting these final words of Jesus to His church, Luke reveals to his readers his primary intent in writing Acts.[31] And by extension, he provides the church of his day (and ultimately the church of every day until Jesus returns) with both its statement of mission and its mandate for ministry. These were to be the church's marching orders until He return- ed to earth (Acts 1:9-11). This dominical promise of Jesus re- veals the overarching theme of the book of Acts: *in order for the church to effectively fulfill Christ's mandate to take the gospel to the ends of the earth, it must remain fully committed to His mission and supernaturally enabled by the Holy Spirit.*

Far too often, however, in our narrow focus on the second half of the verse ("... in Jerusalem and in all Judea and Samaria, and to the end of the earth"), we have missed the greater significance of the first half ("But you will receive power when the Holy Spirit has come upon you, and you will be my wit-

---

[30] In my book, *Empowered for Global Mission: A Missionary Look at the Book of Acts,* I present a comprehensive argument as to why Acts 1:8 should serve as the "interpretative key" for the book (Springfield, MO: Life Publishers, 2005, 77-87).

[31] He does this, however, not propositionally, as did John in his gospel (John 20:31) and first epistle (1 John 5:13), but narratively, using the words of Jesus in His departing promise (and injunction) to his church in Acts 1:8.

nesses...."). This amazing promise of Jesus introduces a motif, or literary pattern, that will be repeated many times throughout the book of Acts. Elsewhere I have called this pattern Luke's *empowerment-witness motif.* This motif is seen most notably in seven key outpourings of the Spirit which occur at significant junctures in the book.[32]

For years cessationist scholars have argued that Luke wrote Acts with purely *historical* intent, having no theological purpose whatsoever. In more recent years, however, this viewpoint has been challenged and largely discounted.[33] Most contemporary Lukan scholars believe that, in addition to writing with historical intent, Luke wrote with clear *theological* intent. Others, myself included, take this idea a step further,

---

[32] I deal with these seven outpourings at length in chapters 4-10 of my book, *Empowered for Global Mission,* pages 91-251. Those seven outpourings are (1) Pentecost, the First Jerusalem Outpouring (2:1-4), (2) the Second Jerusalem Outpouring (4:31), (3) the Samaritan Outpouring (8:14-17), (4) the Damascene Outpouring (9:15-18), (5) the Caesarean Outpouring (10:44-48), (6) the Antiochain "Outpouring" (13:1-3), and (7) the Ephesian Outpouring (19:1-7).

[33] See William W. Menzies and Robert P. Menzies, "Chapter 2: Hermeneutics: The Quiet Revolution" in *Spirit and Power: Foundations of Pentecostal Experience* (Grand Rapids, MI: Zondervan, 2000, 41-44). See also I. Howard I. Marshall, *Luke Historian and Theologian* (Grand Rapids: Zondervan, 1970), and William W. Klein, Craig L. Blomberg, and Robert L. Hubbard, Jr., *Introduction to Biblical Interpretation* (Nashville, TN: W Publishing Group, 1993, 349-350).

believing that Luke wrote primarily with *missiological,* intent as is clearly indicated in Acts 1:8.[34]

The question then arises, how does all of this apply to the subject at hand, that is, the missiological significance of speaking in tongues? A clear understanding of Luke's missional intent in writing Acts will provide us with the necessary context for understanding how Luke presents the practice of speaking tongues in his book.

The Meaning of Pentecost

Pentecost is not essentially about speaking tongues, nor is it about how to be saved. Admittedly, both of these experiences (the first emphasized by Pentecostal interpreters and the second emphasized by non-Pentecostal interpreters) are essential elements of the Pentecostal event. They are not, however, what the narrative is fundamentally about. In Acts Luke presents Pentecost as a direct fulfillment of Jesus' promise in 1:8: "But you will receive power when the Holy Spirit has come upon you, and you will be my witnesses ..." Consequently, Pentecost is primarily about how disciples can be empowered by the Holy Spirit to be Christ's witnesses "in Jerusalem, and in all Judea and Samaria, and to the ends of the earth." While Luke includes many other important details in his narrative, it is essential that we not miss this overarching theme of Spirit-empowered

---

[34] I. Howard Marshall, *New Testament Theology: Many Witnesses One Gospel* (Downers Grove, IL: IVP Academic, 2004). Marshall writes, "Of all the books of the New Testament it is Acts that most clearly exemplifies the relationship of the theology of the early church to its mission. Acts is the story of a mission, in the course of which we learn the theological content of the gospel and the theology on which the mission to Jews and Gentiles rested" (157).

witness. To miss this is to miss the central meaning of Pentecost, and thus the meaning and purpose of the Pentecostal experience, as well as its concomitant sign of speaking in tongues.

Thus, if we are to correctly understand Luke's missional view of tongues, it is essential that we not miss the symbiotic literary connection he makes between Jesus' final promise in Acts 1:8 and the disciples' initial reception of the Spirit in 2:4. Understanding this connection is key to understanding what is happening to the 120 disciples when they were "all filled with the Holy Spirit and began to speak in other tongues as the Spirit gave them utterance."

Because we often read Acts in a disjointed manner, we miss this connection. If, however, one thoughtfully reads chapters 1 and 2 without pause, the cause-and-effect relationship between the two verses becomes apparent.[35] Once this relationship is understood, it becomes further apparent that Luke expected his readers to interpret the tongues spoken by the disciples in 2:4 (and by extension the tongues spoken in 10:46 and 19:6) missiologically. In other words, Luke intended 2:4 to be seen as the direct fulfillment of 1:8!

Therefore, when the disciples on the Day of Pentecost "began to speak in other tongues as the Holy Spirit gave them utterance" they were doing so in fulfillment of Jesus' promise that "you will receive power when the Holy Spirit has come upon you, and you will be my witnesses in Jerusalem and in all Judea and Samaria, and to the end of the earth." Powerful

---

[35] Only 15 parenthetical verses (Acts 1:12-26) separate the story of Jesus' ascension and the Spirit's decent at Pentecost. They tell the story of the disciples' prayerful preparation for Pentecost and of their choosing a replacement for Judas.

missional implications flow from one's understanding of this truth, which I will discuss at length in the following chapters. For now, we should be aware that Luke wrote his narrative concerning the beginnings and missionary advance of the early church with clear missiological intent, and in this context he clearly viewed speaking in tongues as a missional occurrence.

Theology with Feet

More than four decades ago Martin Kähler first declared that "mission is the mother of theology,"[36] implying that all true theology emerges out of mission and that its ultimate purpose is to enable the same. The supreme function of theology, then, is to help us to know God and to serve His purposes more perfectly. Is not this the primary reason that God has revealed Himself to us in Scripture?[37] Any theology, therefore, that does not lead to mission must be reevaluated and remediated. This is because insipid theology leads to insipid practice, and conversely, robust missional theology leads (at least potentially) to robust missions practice. Unfortunately however, Classical Pentecostalism's current non-missional theology of tongues has, in my opinion, negatively impacted the church and

---

[36] Martin Kähler, *Schriften zur Christologie und Mission* (1971, 190). translated by David Bosch in *Transforming Mission: Paradigm Shifts in Theology of Mission* (Maryknoll, NY: Orbis Books, 1991).

[37] Christopher J. H. Wright, *The Mission of God: Unlocking the Bible's Grand Narrative* (Downers Grove, IL: IVP Academic, 2006, 48-51). Wright states, "... the whole canon of Scripture is a missional phenomenon in the sense that it witnesses to the self-giving movement of God toward his creation ... The writings that now comprise our Bible are themselves the product of and witness to the ultimate mission of God" (48).

how it carries out its missionary mandate in the world.

The late missionary-theologian John V. York used to talk of "theology with feet," that is, theology that inspired and enabled effective participation in fulfilling the *missio Dei* (mission of God), and by extension, the *missio ecclesia* (mission of the church).[38] While the early Pentecostal emphasis on *xenolalia* lacked adequate theological and practical groundings, it was, nevertheless, a theology with feet. It captured, at least in part, the missional essence of Luke's perspective on tongues and inspired participants to leave the Azusa Street Mission and other early centers of Pentecostal revival and go quickly to the field. Gary B. McGee has noted that "by 1910 some 185 Pentecostal missionaries had been marshaled over a four-year period from the outset of the 1906-1909 Azusa Street Revival." He further noted that from Azusa Street "a new missiological paradigm would emerge for the twentieth century."[39]

While, as stated above, I am not calling for a return to the xenolalic missionary tongues of Parham and Seymour, I am calling for is a fresh look at the missional nature of tongues as presented by Luke in the book of Acts. The time is ripe for the

---

[38] In his book, *Missions in the Age of the Spirit*, York also discusses the issues of Spirit baptism and tongues in missions (Springfield, MO: Gospel Publishing House, 1999, 181-187).

[39] Gary B. McGee, "Missions, Overseas (North America)" in *Dictionary of Pentecostal and Charismatic Movements,* eds. Stanley M. Burgess and Gary B. McGee (Grand Rapids, MI: Regency Reference Library, Zondervan Publishing House, 1988, 612), quoted in Denzil R. Miller, *From Azusa to Africa to the Nations* (Springfield, MO: Assemblies of God World Missions: Africa Office, 2005, 22).

Pentecostal movement to reevaluate and remediate its narrow, non-missional "tongues-as-a-heavenly-prayer-language" theological emphasis bequeathed to it by the Charismatic Renewal of the 1960's. It must also abandon its recently-acquired reticence to fully embrace and encourage the practice of speaking in tongues in its churches, a reticence engendered, at least in part, by the emergence of the "tongues-as-a-non-essential-option" theology of the Third Wave movement. Additionally, it is high time for Pentecostals to fortify their long-held, yet in many ways missionally-deficient, initial physical evidence doctrine with the fuller and more missionally-robust theology of speaking in tongues as presented by Luke in the book of Acts. At this divinely-appointed moment in salvation history, the Pentecostal church must (re)discover Luke's "tongues-as-missional-empowerment" theology as presented in the book of Acts.

Before I proceed any further, another clarification is in order. In advocating a return to Luke's missional presentation of tongues, I am by no means writing in opposition to the idea of tongues as a means of intercession and adoration as presented in the Pauline epistles (Rom. 8:26-27; 1 Cor. 14:16-17; Eph. 5:18-19) and in the gospel of Luke (10:21). These practices must be embraced and encouraged in the churches. I am simply saying that, while these understandings are, in and of themselves, true enough, apart from Luke's missional understanding of tongues, they are an egregiously inadequate and potentially debilitating view of the missionally dynamic practice of speaking in tongues.

Pentecostalism's wholesale adoption of the Pauline "heavenly-prayer-language" orientation, to the exclusion of Luke's "tongues-as-missional-empowerment" orientation concerning speaking in tongues, has lessened the impact of Spirit baptism in the lives of many Christians and in the evangelistic and missionary enterprise of the church. Unfortunately, in far too many contemporary Pentecostal circles Spirit baptism is understood as a cathartic spiritual experience resulting in a prayer language rather than as a powerful, life-altering spiritual experience accompanied by missional tongues and resulting in Spirit-empowered witness to the lost, as the experience is so clearly portrayed by Luke in the book of Acts.

New Interpretative Approaches

The emergence of new interpretative disciplines during the past three decades has enabled Pentecostal scholars to demonstrate exegetically what early Pentecostal scholars perceived intuitively. The disciplines of biblical and narrative theology have enhanced the church's understanding of Luke's unique presentation of the work of the Spirit in missions. Out of these disciplines has risen the field of Lukan Pneumatology. Using these interpretative approaches, Pentecostal scholars have been able to more clearly articulate the nature and purpose of Spirit baptism and to fortify their prophetic and missional view of the experience. They have been able to convincingly demonstrate how Luke's pneumatology is essentially prophetic and missional.[40] He writes, not to teach how the Spirit regenerates repentant sinners and initiates them into new covenant exis-

---

[40] Significant contributions have been made by, among others, Roger Stronstad (*The Charismatic Theology of St. Luke,* 1984), James B. Shelton (*Mighty in Word in Deed,* 1991), and Robert P. Menzies (*Empowered for Witness,* 2001). I have also written on the topic in *Empowered for Global Mission* (2005).

tence, as some have contended,[41] but to show how the Spirit empowers believers to bear prophetic (that is, Spirit-empowered) witness at home and to the ends of the earth.

Among other things, biblical theologians insist that the voice of each biblical author should be clearly heard and uniquely understood. That is, the distinctive message of one biblical writer should not be lost by arbitrarily superimposing that of another upon him. Each biblical author should be allowed to speak out of his own historical context and in alignment with his own purpose in writing. In other words, Luke's pneumatology of empowerment should not be held hostage to Paul's more soteriological emphasis.

Biblical theologians have rightly noted that when one takes this more common sense approach to interpreting Scripture, a richer, fuller understanding emerges, one that incorporates both Luke's and Paul's unique pneumatological emphases. Interestingly enough, early Pentecostals were among the first to theologically liberate Luke from Paul, and to more clearly hear Luke's missional voice (although they would have never used this terminology).

Two Writers, Two Perspectives

What Pentecostal exegetes have failed to do, however, is to adequately address the crucial theological connection Luke makes between speaking in tongues and mission. This failure

---

[41] Most notably James D. G. Dunn in *Baptism in the Holy Spirit: A Re-examination of the New Testament Teaching on the Gift of the Spirit in Relation to Pentecostalism Today* (Philadelphia: The Westminster Press, 1970), and John R. W. Stott in *Baptism and Fullness of the Holy Spirit* (Downers Grove, IL: Inter-Varsity Press, 1964).

has, in my opinion, been a "missing ingredient" in the Pentecostal understanding of the nature and purpose of the experience of Spirit baptism—and of its accompanying sign of speaking in tongues. More importantly, this failure to properly explain the missional nature of tongues has mitigated the missional impact of the experience on the lives and ministries of Spirit-filled Christians, and has helped to devalue the experience in the minds of many contemporary Pentecostals.

What is often overlooked in the ongoing discussion about speaking in tongues is the fact that while both Paul and Luke are indeed speaking of the same spiritual phenomenon, they are nevertheless speaking out of different contexts and thus writing with different purposes in mind.

Paul's congregational context. In 1 Corinthians 12-14 Paul is writing to a dissonant church seeking to bring its members back into Christian harmony. The church's disunity is being exacerbated by their misuse of spiritual gifts in their congregational gatherings—especially the gift of tongues. Paul writes to instruct the church concerning the proper function of the gifts when the congregation gathers for spiritual worship.[42] He further uses the opportunity to bring the Corinthian believers into a more perfect understanding of the proper exercise of tongues in both congregational worship and in private prayer. Although he never loses sight of the fact that true worship does indeed have evangelistic implications (14:24-45), his primary purpose in writing is not to encourage the church to reach the lost, but to bring members back into loving unity. In other

---

[42] The congregational context of his instructions to the Corinthian church concerning spiritual gifts is demonstrated by his repetitive use of the phrase "when the church comes together" (cf. 1 Cor. 11:17-18, 20, 33;14:23, 26).

words, Paul is not so much concerned with the operation of spiritual gifts in the church scattered in frontline evangelism as he is their use in the church gathered for sacred worship. His teaching on tongues thus reflects Paul's concerns and motives in writing.[43]

While it is essential that we clearly understand and carefully apply Paul's congregationally-oriented teaching concerning the proper uses of the gift of tongues to the practice of the church gathered in worship, we must do this with the full understanding that Paul's teachings do not tell the full story. In order to get a complete picture of New Testament teaching on tongues, we must also hear from Luke on the subject, and we must allow him to speak out his own missional context and with his unique missional purposes in mind.

Luke's missional context. Luke presents tongues in a significantly different context than does Paul, and he writes with a different purpose in mind. While Paul wrote about tongues in the context of the church gathered in worship, and his chief concerns were correctional and edificational, Luke discusses tongues in the context of the church scattered in frontline evangelism and missions, and his primary concern is the missionary expansion of the church. His teaching on tongues thus reflects this missional context and concern.

---

[43] From Paul's teachings in 1 Corinthians and Romans, Pentecostal/Charismatic Christians have developed a number of concepts and practices involving speaking in tongues, including tongues as a heavenly prayer language (1 Cor 13:1; 14:1,4-15), tongues as a congregational gift (1 Cor. 12:10; 28), tongues as a means of congregational edification (1 Cor. 14:12-13, 26), tongues as a means of personal edification (14:4), tongues as a means of Spirit-inspired praise and worship (1 Cor. 14:15-17), and tongues as a means of intercessory prayer in the Spirit (Rom. 12:26-27).

Writing from around A.D. 65 to 70, more than thirty years after the initial outpouring of the Spirit on the Day of Pentecost, Luke wrote to a second generation of Christians, many of whom were not alive when the early events of Acts occurred. They likely lived remotely from Jerusalem, and reasoning from the book's internal evidence, it appears that Luke's original readers were predominantly Gentiles and hellenized Jews. Also, from the book's internal evidence we deduce that the people to whom Luke was writing were undergoing severe persecution, and as a result, there was a waning missionary vision among them.[44] Further, gauging from Luke's strong missiopneumatic emphasis in Acts, there seems to have been an accompanying de-emphasis on the empowering work of the Spirit in their community.

Luke thus wrote to these second generation Christians to call them back to the church's Pentecostal and missionary roots. By telling his readers the story of the Spirit-empowered missionary advance of the early church, he hoped to convince them that any community of believers, even if they are enduring great persecution, can be a force in the earth—if they will be empowered by the Spirit and remain committed to God and

---

[44] Effective Spirit-empowered witness in the face of ongoing persecution is a major recurring theme in the book of Acts. Luke records at least 28 instances of persecution, including opposition (11:1-3; 13:8, 45; 14:4-7; 15:2), threats (4:18-21; 5:27-28; 5:33-40; 9:1; 14:4-7; 22:24), mocking (17:32), reviling (18:6), false accusations (8:12-13), plots (9:23-25; 23:12-15), arrests (4:3; 9:2, 13-14; 21:30-36), imprisonment (4:3; 5:17-18; 8:3; 12:3-5; 16:22-24), stoning (7:58-60; 14:19); ravaging (8:3), banishment (8:1; 13:50-52; 17:13-14), beating (16:22-24), unprovoked attacks (17:5-9), false trials (23:23–24:27; 25:1-12: 25:13-26:32), and murder (12:1-2). In every instance the church perseveres and advances in the power of the Spirit.

His mission.[45] It seems reasonable, therefore, as we seek to understand Luke's presentation of tongues in the book of Acts, that we take into account the strong missionary context in which they occur.

Unfortunately, few Pentecostal exegetes have made this missional connection. This failure has significantly affected the way modern Pentecostals view Spirit baptism, along with the way they view its cognate practice of speaking in tongues. Not only has today's Pentecostal church significantly lost Luke's missio-pneumatic understanding of the Spirit's work in the believer and in the church, in the century since the movement began the Pentecostal church has all but abandoned the early Pentecostals' missional emphasis concerning speaking in tongues. The present prevailing Pentecostal understanding concerning tongues has shifted away from a predominantly Lukan empowerment emphasis to a predominantly Pauline edificational emphasis. While most Pentecostal scholars and pastors understand and teach that Spirit baptism has clear missionary implications, few see the missional nature and purposes of speaking in tongues.

In the following chapters I will address this issue. I will seek to develop (or at least begin to develop) a fuller, more missional understanding of how Luke presents speaking in tongues in the book of Acts. In doing this I will argue that in Acts Luke presents speaking in tongues in at least four distinct ways: (1) as a confirmatory evidence, (2) as a missional sign, (3) as a prophetic release, and (4) as enabling element.

---

[45] In the first chapter of my book, *Empowered for Global Mission,* "Interpreting Acts," I discuss the issue of Luke's intent in writing Acts at some length (25-53).

CHAPTER 3

LUKE'S MISSIONAL PRESENTATION OF TONGUES

PART 1:
TONGUES AS A CONFIRMATORY EVIDENCE

ACTS 10:45-46

*And the believers from among the circumcised
who had come with Peter were amazed,
because the gift of the Holy Spirit was poured out
even on the Gentiles.
For they were hearing them speaking in tongues
and extolling God.*

In his inspired history of the early church, Luke mentions speaking in tongues three times (Acts 2:4; 10:46; 19:6). It is from these three occurrences, along with two instances where speaking in tongues can be logically deduced (8:16-19; 9:17-18 with 1 Cor. 14:18), that Pentecostals have developed their tenet of evidential tongues. While this is good, as we proceed through our study it is important that we not miss two other essential facts concerning speaking in tongues in Acts. The first, as I have already mentioned, is that in each of these occurrences Luke presents speaking in tongues as part of a direct fulfillment of Jesus' final promise to His church in Acts 1:8: "But you will receive power when the Holy Spirit has come upon you; and you will be my witnesses in Jerusalem, and in all Judea and Samaria, and to the end of the earth." Secondly, we must be aware of how Luke strategically places each of these "pneuma events" in his narrative in order to showcase how each helps to advance his missio-pneumatic intent in writing Acts.[46]

It is therefore not without significance that each time Luke mentions speaking in tongues in Acts, he prefaces the occurrence by reiterating the "coming upon" metaphor first used by Jesus in Acts 1:8: "But you will receive power when the Holy Spirit has *come upon* you ..." (cf. 2:3; 10:44; 19:6). In doing this he is linguistically alerting his readers to what is actually happening to the disciples in each instance. The Spirit is coming upon them to implement Christ's twofold promise of 1:8 into their lives. By being filled with the Spirit *and* speaking in tongues the disciples are receiving power that they might be Christ's witnesses to the ends of the earth. I will expand on this concept in Chapter 5.

---

[46] These are three of seven key outpourings of the Spirit in Acts. In *Empowered for Global Witness* I discuss at length how these seven outpourings of the Spirit are essential to understanding the central message and flow of the book of Acts.

Tongues as a Confirmatory Evidence

One way Luke presents speaking in tongues in Acts is as a unique confirmatory evidence (or verifying witness) to one's having received the Spirit as promised by Jesus in Acts 1:8. He does this implicitly in two instances (Acts 2:4; 19:6) and explicitly in another (10:45-46).

Historically speaking, at Pentecost tongues were unarguably *the* initial sign that the Holy Spirit had indeed come upon Christ's disciples, filled them, and given them power to be His witnesses to the nations (cf. Acts 1:4-8). On that occasion the 120 "were all filled with the Holy Spirit and began to speak in other tongues as the Spirit gave them utterance" (2:4). In this straightforward declaration Luke infers a clear cause-and-effect relationship between the disciples' receiving the Spirit and their Spirit-enabled speaking in tongues—a relationship He does not want his readers to miss. The same causal relationship is implied in 19:6: "And when Paul had laid his hands on them, the Holy Spirit came on them, and they began speaking in tongues and prophesying."

While in each of the two above incidences (2:4 and 19:6) Luke's "evidential connection" between Spirit baptism and speaking in tongues is strongly inferred, in his third instance, the outpouring of the Spirit on the household of Cornelius in Caesarea, the connection is explicitly stated (10:45-46). In describing this outpouring Luke clearly states that speaking in tongues was the confirmatory evidence that these Gentile believers had authentically received the Spirit just as had the 120 Jews in Jerusalem a few weeks earlier on the Day of Pentecost (11:14-17; cf. 15:8). Luke notes that the Jewish believers who accompanied Peter to Caesarea knew that the Gentiles had received the Holy Spirit "for (Greek, *gar,* "because") they were hearing them speaking in tongues and extolling God" (10:46).

Commenting on Luke's illative use of the word *gar,* Robert W. Graves states, "Only a divinely assigned cause-effect pattern would justify Luke's use of *gar* in Acts 10:46 and explain the unargued acceptance of the Gentiles simply because they had praised God in other tongues."[47] Thus, in this parenthetical aside Luke explains to his readers how Peter's Jewish companions knew that the Gentiles had received the Spirit.[48] It was because they were hearing them speaking with tongues and exalting God. In all probability Luke deliberately inserted this explanatory comment so that his readers would know that they too could expect to speak in tongues and exalt God (i.e., bear Spirit-inspired witness) when they were baptized in the Holy Spirit.[49] This passage represents Luke's clearest example of tongues serving as an evidence of disciples' having received the Spirit. The Gentiles' speaking in tongues witnessed to and verified the fact that they had received the Spirit (in the same way and for the same purpose) as had the 120 on the Day of Pentecost (11:15-17).

Initial Evidence

---

[47] Robert W. Graves, "The Use of gar in Acts 10:46," *Paraclete* 22, no. 2 (Spring 1988), 15-18.

[48] In *Empowered for Global Mission* I discuss Luke's use of parenthetical commentary in Acts (45-48).

[49] In *Empowered for Global Mission* I contend that the "extolling God" in 10:46 and the "prophecy" in 19:6 both refer to the same kind of Spirit-inspired witness that took place at Pentecost. This witness occurred in both known and unknown languages (190-194).

Classical Pentecostals have historically employed the phrase "initial physical evidence" to describe this verificational function of speaking in tongues.[50] In advancing their distinctive doctrine they have noted a clear, repeated pattern in the book of Acts. In each of the five instances where individuals are initially baptized in the Spirit, sequent speaking in tongues is either explicitly stated (2:4; 10:46; 19:6) or strongly implied (8:16-17; 9:17 with 1 Cor. 14:4). Based on this inductive approach to Scripture, Classical Pentecostals have historically contended that this pattern constitutes a clear, prescriptive precedent and should therefore serve as a normative model for receiving the Spirit until Jesus returns from heaven.

Non-Pentecostal scholars have challenged this doctrinal formulation on hermeneutical grounds, claiming that it is an illegitimate use of New Testament historical narrative.[51] The Pentecostal use of historical precedent in forming normative teaching has further been challenged by Pentecostal insider, Gordon D. Fee, who asserts that "unless Scripture explicitly tells us we must do something, what is only narrated or described does not function in a normative (i.e., obligatory)

---

[50] The Assemblies of God "Statement of Fundamental Truths" uses the phrase "initial physical sign" to describe the doctrine. In their "Official Declaration of Faith," the Church of God, International of Cleveland, Tennessee, uses the term "initial evidence."

[51] Significant challenges have come from John R. W. Stott in *Baptism and Fullness of the Holy Spirit* (Downers Grove, IL: Inter-Varsity Press, 1964) and James D. G. Dunn, *Baptism in the Holy Spirit: A Re-examination of the New Testament Teaching on the Gift of the Spirit in Relation to Pentecostalism Today* (Philadelphia, PA: Westminster Press, 1970).

way—*unless it can be demonstrated on other grounds that the author intended it to function in this way*" (italics in the original).[52] He further insists that "God's word *for us* in narrative is primarily related to what it was *intended* to teach."[53] He then contends that the distinctive Pentecostal doctrines of subsequence and evidential tongues fail to rise to this standard, and therefore cannot be considered as normative. I believe that the use of Fee's books in Pentecostal Bible and extension schools around the world has served to significantly weaken the belief in normative tongues in the minds of many Pentecostal pastors and leaders.

In more recent times, through the application of the disciplines of biblical and narrative theology, contemporary Pentecostal scholars have strengthened their arguments concerning the Pentecostal doctrines of subsequence and normative evidential tongues.[54] Notwithstanding, in this ongoing debate between Pentecostal and non-Pentecostal scholars one thing cannot be denied, in Acts 10:45-46 Luke clearly presents tongues as the verificational sign which convinced Peter's six

---

[52] Gordon D. Fee and Douglas Stuart, "Acts–The Problem of Historical Precedent" in *How to Read the Bible for All Its Worth: A Guide to Understanding the Bible,* 3rd ed. (Grand Rapids, MI: Zondervan, 2003), 118-119.

[53] Ibid., 121.

[54] Those scholars include, among others, Howard M. Ervin (1971), Roger Stronstad (1984), French L. Arrington (1988), Robert P. Menzies (1991), and James Shelton (1991). I discuss these scholars' responses to the challenges leveled against Pentecostal teaching in *Implications of Lukan Pneumatology: Doctoral Study Guide,* PTH901, 6th ed. (Lome, Togo: Pan-Africa Theological Seminary, 2013), 22-59.

Jewish companions—as well as "the apostles and bothers" in Jerusalem—that the Gentiles in Caesarea had, in truth, received the Spirit just as they had first received Him on the Day of Pentecost (10:45-46; cf. 11:15-18). In this passage Luke unambiguously presents speaking in tongues as a confirmatory evidence that one has been filled with the Holy Spirit.

Further implications flow from the early Pentecostals' careful framing of the phrase "initial physical evidence" to describe their distinctive doctrine. The word *initial* implies that, along with speaking in tongues, one can expect other ensuant evidences of having received the Spirit.[55] The word *physical* implies that, in addition to the outward physical manifestation of speaking in tongues, there is a corresponding inner spiritual work taking place in the heart of the receiver, including powerful inner spiritual transformation. I will discuss these ideas more in Chapters 5 and 6.

Voices of Dissent—Voices of Approbation

In recent years voices of dissent have arisen from within the movement calling for Pentecostals to abandon their historic stance on evidential tongues in favor of a more ecumenically palatable formulation. Some are calling for a presentation of

---

[55] The Assemblies of God "Statement of Fundamental Truths, Section 7, 'Baptism in the Holy Spirit'" states, "With it [Spirit baptism] comes the enduement of power for life and service, the bestowment of the gifts and their uses in the work of ministry (Luke 24:49; Acts 1:4, 8; 1 Cor. 12:1-31).... With the baptism in the Holy Spirit come such experiences as: an overflowing fullness of the Spirit (John 7:37-39; Acts 4:8), a deepened reverence for God (Acts 2:43; Heb. 12:28); an intensified consecration to God and dedication to His work (Acts 2:42); and a more active love for Christ, for His Word, and for the lost (Mark 16:20)."

tongues that does not directly link the practice with Spirit baptism and does not rigidly demand that every believer actively seek the gift of the Spirit evidenced by speaking in tongues. These advocates seek a more "user-friendly" Pentecostalism that more nearly mirrors the ethos of the prevailing pluralistic culture. This desire has been buoyed, at least in part, by the emergence of the less confrontational Third Wave presentation of Spirit baptism that frames the experience in terms of "completion" or "actualization"[56] rather than in terms of a *"donum superadditum"* as is held by traditional Pentecostals.[57] Third Wave teachers further present speaking in tongues in less prescriptive Pauline categories (i.e., tongues as a gift for some) rather than the more prescriptive Lukan categories (i.e., tongues as a normative missional sign for all who have received the empowering gift of the Spirit).

Pentecostals would, nonetheless, be ill-advised to abandon

---

[56] John Wimber, *Power Evangelism* (New York: Harper and Row Publishers, 1986). Wimber writes, "Anyone born again has the potential of experiencing the power and gifts of the Holy Spirit.... As Christians learn that there is more to experience, they are willing to take a chance, step out in faith, and receive God's power.... I tell them that all that remains is to *actualize* what the Spirit has, all that is required is to release the gifts" (147-148). See also, Phil Strout, *Core Values and Beliefs,* www.vineyarduse.org (accessed January 20, 2014).

[57] Robert P. Menzies, *Empowered for Witness: Studies in Luke-Acts* (Sheffield, ENG: Sheffield, 2001). According to Menzies, in Acts "the disciples receive the Spirit as a prophetic *donum superadditum* which enables them to participate effectively in the missionary enterprise of the church" (227). A *donum superadditum* is a gift from God graciously added to one that has already been given.

this core teaching of their movement, for much more is at stake than simply maintaining a Pentecostal tradition. Such a course redirection would, I believe, inevitably result in unintended, and possibly irreparable, damage to the movement. Most significantly, a redefining of the Pentecostal doctrine of evidential tongues would diminish the church's effectiveness in carrying out its God-ordained mission of taking the gospel to the ends of the earth before the soon coming of Christ. In the following chapters I will discuss in more detail how speaking in tongues as presented by Luke in the book of Acts has profound missional implications.

Further, if the Pentecostal church in the West were to abandon its historical stance on evidential tongues, such a move would most certainly negatively impact its relationship with its sister Pentecostal churches in the Global South where the vast majority of Pentecostals now reside. The Global South church has far less ambivalence on the subject than does the church in the Global North. For instance, every African Pentecostal leader with whom I have interfaced in the last fifteen years holds firmly to the Classical Pentecostal position that every believer who is genuinely baptized in the Holy Spirit will speak in tongues as the Spirit enables.[58]

This fact is aptly demonstrated by the Decade of Pentecost

---

[58] In my travels throughout Africa during the past 15 years I have met personally with leaders of national Assemblies of God churches in 32 separate nations. Not one had any reservations about speaking in tongues being the initial physical evidence of one's being baptized in the Holy Spirit. One candidly stated, "If you Pentecostals in America have doubts concerning the doctrine of initial evidence, please keep them to yourselves. We don't need your doubts in Africa!"

emphasis launched by the Africa Assemblies of God Alliance (AAGA) stretching from Pentecost Sunday 2010 to Pentecost Sunday 2020. AAGA is a vast network of 17 million AG adherents meeting in 71 thousand local churches affiliated with 50 national churches in sub-Sahara Africa and the Indian Ocean Basin.[59] During those ten years the Africa AG have set a collective goal of seeing 10 million new believers baptized in the Holy Spirit and then mobilized as Spirit-empowered witnesses, church planters, and cross-cultural missionaries to the unreached tribes of Africa and beyond.[60] The expectation is that every one of these believers will be empowered by the Spirit and speak in tongues as the Spirit gives utterance according to the promise of Jesus (Acts 1:8) and the pattern of Pentecost (2:4). Already churches are reporting that tens of thousands have been baptized in the Holy Spirit evidenced by speaking in tongues. More reports are coming into our Acts in Africa offices on an almost daily basis.

If the Pentecostal church of the West were to moderate its historic stance concerning evidential tongues, such an action would inevitably drive a theological and methodological wedge between them and their Global South counterparts. Even in those instances where cordial relationships would be maintained, the Pentecostal ambivalence of the missionaries sent

---

[59] The Assemblies of God, USA, "Africa Statistics" report ending December 31, 2012 indicates that the Africa AG has 17,768,140 adherents in 71,445 churches and preaching points with 75,974 ministers (General Council of the Assemblies of God, Statistical Office, Springfield, MO, December 31, 2013).

[60] Website: www.DecadeofPentecost.org (accessed Dec. 20 2013).

from the West would surely influence and negatively impact their host churches around the world. Such an impact would consequently diminish the effectiveness of their emerging church planting and missionary movements.

The late missionary statesman, John V. York, understood the symbiotic relationship between tongues and mission. He appealed to the Pentecostal church to not abandon its historic emphasis on speaking in tongues:

> As long as there is a hurting and broken world divided primarily along lines of language and ethnicity, I hope Pentecostals will increase their emphasis upon speaking in tongues. It would be an untold tragedy to back away from that part of our heritage that most directly gives evidence of God's determination to bless all nations through Christ the seed of Abraham (Gal. 3:6).[61]

In a paper presented to the Society for Pentecostal Studies in 1993, church historian Vinson Synan issued a similar admonition. After reviewing the pivotal role that the doctrine of normative evidential tongues has played in the development and growth of modern Pentecostalism, Synan exhorted the gathered delegates,

> In the end, the teaching of tongues as initial evidence has played a major role in recent church history. The Pentecostal experience and the doctrine explaining it has galvanized the most explosive movement among Christians since the days of the Reformation. It is unthinkable that the Pentecostal movement could have developed as it did without

---

[61] John V. York, *Missions in the Age of the Spirit* (Springfield, MO: Gospel Publishing House, 2000), 186.

the initial evidence position.[62]

This being said, while the twenty-first century Pentecostal church must remain firmly committed to its doctrine of initial evidence, it must also realize that this teaching is only a partial understanding of Luke's missional presentation of tongues in Acts. All too often, in their zeal to defend their Pentecostal distinctive, Pentecostals have overlooked other important Lukan emphases concerning speaking in tongues in Acts. As a result, the missional impact of the experience has not been fully realized in the lives of most present-day recipients of the Pentecostal gift. This fact is especially evident when one juxtaposes the comparative pallid affect of the experience on the lives of modern Pentecostals with the affect of the experience on the early disciples as recorded by Luke in the book of Acts.

During this pivotal moment in the missionary history of the modern Pentecostal movement, it is essential that we Pentecostals come to grips with the fact that in the book of Acts Luke presents speaking in tongues as much more than an initial physical evidence. Further, we must collectively acknowledge that, in and of itself, our Classical Pentecostal formulation concerning speaking in tongues has failed to adequately capture Luke's intentioned missional presentation of the experience. As presently formulated and popularly taught, the doctrine neither theologically nor practically points us toward the harvest as, I believe, Luke envisioned it would do. In other

---

[62] Vinson Synan, "The Role of Tongues as Initial Evidence," in *Conference Papers on the Theme, To the Ends of the Earth, Presented at the Twenty-third Annual Meeting of the Society for Pentecostal Studies* (November 11-13, 1993), 18.

words, our current, popular teaching concerning evidential tongues lacks the "missiological feet" needed to help mobilize the church to effectively penetrate today's missions frontiers.

As I have already emphasized, I am not suggesting that Pentecostals abandon our distinctive teaching on initial evidence. God forbid that we should make that grievous mistake! What I am suggesting, however, it that we must fortify this teaching with a fuller, more missional—and I would add, a more biblical—understanding of speaking in tongues as presented by Luke in the book of Acts. While the movement must reaffirm its historic doctrine, it must be willing to boldly move beyond it. This I will attempt to do in the following three chapters.

CHAPTER 4

LUKE'S MISSIONAL PRESENTATION OF TONGUES

PART 2:
TONGUES AS A MISSIONAL SIGN

ACTS 2:4, 7-8

*And they were all filled with the Holy Spirit
and began to speak in other tongues
as the Spirit gave them utterance.
... And they were amazed and astonished,
saying, "Are not all these who are speaking
Galileans? And how is it that we hear,
each of us in his own native language?"*

A Missional Sign

Not only does Luke present tongues as a confirming evidence of one's having been baptized in the Holy Spirit, as discussed in the last chapter, he also presents them as a missional sign, pointing to the fuller meaning of the experience.

He does this in his Pentecost account by carefully crafting his narrative to emphasize, not only the missional nature of the gift of the Spirit, but the missional nature of the sign accompanying it. For instance, after describing the disciples' Spirit-enabled speaking in tongues in Acts 2:4, Luke immediately informs his readers, "Now there were dwelling in Jerusalem Jews, devout men from every nation under heaven" (v. 5). He then lists 15 Gentile languages spoken by those who had just received the Spirit (vv. 6-11.) His list is reminiscent of Moses' "Table of Nations" found in Genesis 10 representing all the nations of the world. It seems that Luke did not want his readers to miss the fact that the disciples' speaking in tongues at Pentecost was more than a random ecstatic spiritual phenomenon. Neither was it a form of "primal speech," as some have suggested.[63] It was rather a divinely-chosen missional sign. It was, as I have previously mentioned, the direct fulfillment of Jesus' final missionary promise in Acts 1:8 and signified that God was empowering His church (including both the twelve apostles and the 108± other disciples) to proclaim Christ "in Jerusalem and in all Judea and Samaria, and to the end of the earth." In the Markan version of Jesus' Great Commission—a verse often quoted by early Pentecostals—Jesus had already informed the Eleven that speaking in "new tongues" was to be one of the missional signs characterizing the lives and ministries of believers (Mark 16:17).

---

[63] Harvey Cox, *Fire from Heaven: The Rise of Pentecostal Spirituality and the Reshaping of Religion in the Twenty-first Century* (Cambridge, MA: Da Capo Press, 2001), 81-97.

Luke further highlights the missional nature of speaking in tongues in Peter's Pentecost "sermon."[64] There he skillfully uses Peter's Spirit-inspired message to interpret the miraculous events of Pentecost.[65] Even the question from the crowd of onlookers ("What does this mean?") implies that disciples' speaking in tongues carried with it a deeper meaning (v. 12). In this prophetic utterance Peter quotes the ancient Hebrew prophet Joel (2:28-32a). Several times he redacts, or edits, the words of the prophet.[66] The redaction most relevant to our present discussion is found in verse 19. In this verse Peter, inspired by the Holy Spirit, changes Joel's "I will show wonders in the heavens and on the earth" (Joel 2:30) to "I will show wonders in the heavens above *and signs* on the earth below" (emphasis added). Luke thus highlights Peter's addition of the phrase "and signs" to the words of the prophet. In doing this he alerts his readers to the fact that the disciples' speaking in tongues was to be prominent among those last-days "signs on

---

[64] Peter's "sermon" at Pentecost was actually not a sermon at all, at least not in the traditional sense that we understand sermons today. It was rather a prophetic utterance, as will be discussed later in the book.

[65] Luke employed a similar strategy in Luke 4:18-19 where he used Jesus' quotation of Isaiah 61:1-2 to interpret what happened to Jesus when the Spirit came upon Him at His baptism in 3:21-22. Just as He would later do at Pentecost, the Spirit came upon Jesus at the Jordan to anoint and empower Him for mission.

[66] I tend to believe that Peter was the original "redactor" of Joel's words and that Luke is quoting his actual words. The redaction is thus a work of the Spirit as He inspires Peter's prophetic words. Luke then chooses Peter's Spirit-inspired words to advance his own theological and missional agenda in writing Acts.

the earth below." Roger Stronstad comments on the symbol-ic nature of the tongues spoken at Pentecost:

> On the day of Pentecost the disciples, who are to be witnesses (Luke 24:49; Acts 1:8), are endowed with a gift which is symbolic for their task; namely, *they began to speak in other tongues as the Spirit gave utterance.* In other words, as the sign that they have received the power of the Spirit to witness *to the remotest part of the earth* (Acts 1:8) the disciples, filled with the Spirit, speak in tongues or languages of the world (2:9-11), speak in languages other than their native language, speak in languages hitherto unlearned but now momentarily medi-ated to them by the Holy Spirit.[67]

Luke thus presents speaking in tongues as a missional sign indicating that the receiver has been empowered by the Spirit as a last days prophet to the nations.

The Meaning of Tongues in Acts

One function of a sign is to help convey the meaning of the thing it signifies. This is true of the sign of tongues as pre-sented by Luke in Acts. It speaks to the deeper meaning, pur-pose, and nature of the Pentecostal gift. Taken in context, the disciples' speaking in tongues at Pentecost signified that in fulfillment of Jesus' promise they had received power to be Christ's prophetic witnesses "in Jerusalem and in all Judea and Samaria, and to the end of the earth" (Acts 1:8) and to "every tribe and language and people and nation" (Rev. 5:9). In Acts

---

[67] Roger Stronstad, *Signs on the Earth Below: A Commentary on Acts 2:1-21* (Springfield, MO: Life Publishers International, 2003), 29.

tongues appear to signify at least three things:

1. Tongues signify to the recipient that he or she has been empowered to speak for God. When a disciple is filled with the Holy Spirit and speaks in tongues, he or she should understand that this is God's sign to them that they have been empowered to speak prophetically to the lost on Christ's behalf. I like how my friend, Paul York, puts it. He has noted that there are two ways a disciple may bear Christian witness. First, *he can speak to people about God.* This is good, but there is a better way: *God can speak through him to people.* This prophetic, or Spirit-inspired, witness is the kind that Peter bore on the Day of Pentecost. The Spirit first spoke through Peter and the 120 enabling them to speak in tongues (Acts 2:4). He again spoke through Peter enabling Him to effectively proclaim Christ to the lost (2:14-40). In like manner, when one is baptized in the Holy Spirit today and speaks in tongues as the Spirit gives utterance, he or she is encouraged to know that God has empowered and fitted them as vessels through whom He can speak to the lost, effectively proclaiming the message of Christ unto them.

2. Tongues signify to the believing community that they are a last-days, prophetic community. Tongues also serve as a sign to the church. When a gathering of believers hear a new disciple speaking in tongues at his or her Spirit baptism, they are reminded that they are God's last-days, prophetic community called and empowered to bear Christian witness to the nations. They are further reminded that the Spirit is coming on this new disciple just as "he had come on [Peter and the 120] at the beginning" (Acts 11:15, NIV). That is, the Spirit has come upon him or her with the same missional sign and for the same missionary purpose as He came upon the first disciples on the

Day of Pentecost.

In his Pentecost message, Peter uses the prophecy of Joel to explain to the gathered crowd the meaning of what has just occurred. He begins by saying, "This [meaning this outpouring of the Spirit accompanied by speaking in tongues] is that which was spoken [literally, "uttered"] by the prophet Joel" (Acts 2:16, KJV). He continues,

> And in the last days it shall be, God declares, that I will pour out my Spirit on all flesh, and your sons and your daughters *shall prophesy,* and your young men shall see visions, and your old men shall dream dreams; even on my male servants and female servants in those days I will pour out my Spirit, and *they shall prophesy.* (vv. 17-18, emphasis added)

Luke thus identifies the disciples' speaking in tongues as a fulfillment of Joel's prophecy that in the last days all of God's people would become Spirit-inspired prophets. Their speaking in tongues was an eschatological sign heralding the founding of a new last-days prophetic community. And, as if to underscore this fact, he appends a second "and they shall prophesy" to Joel's original prophecy. Additionally, Luke redacts the words of Joel, substituting the phrase "in the last days" for Joel's original "afterward" indicating that this outpouring of the Spirit accompanied by Spirit-inspired languages was an undeniable indication that the last days *(eschatais hemerais)* had dawned.[68]

---

[68] The "Last Days" began with Jesus' first coming in the power of the Spirit (Luke 4:18-19); it will end when He comes again in power and great glory (21:27). During this time Jesus has tasked His church to preach the gospel of the kingdom "throughout the whole world as a testimony to all nations, and then the end will

Joel's prophecy further indicates that this last-days outpouring of the Spirit was to be (at least potentially) universal, that is, it would be upon "all flesh," including sons, daughters, young men, old men, and male and female servants. Some, myself included, believe Pentecost to be the first fulfillment of Moses' wish that "all the LORD's people were prophets, that the LORD would put his Spirit on them!" (Num. 11:29).[69] Roger Stronstad convincingly argues that Pentecost heralded the beginning of the "prophethood of all believers."[70] When a believer speaks in tongues, the gathered community, if they have been properly taught, are reminded that the church is a unique company of last-days, Spirit-empowered prophets called and empowered to take the gospel to the ends of the earth before the soon coming of Christ, and that speaking in tongues is the unique sign of that prophetic community.

Robert P. Menzies cogently sums up this missional reading of tongues in Acts, stating that "tongues calls the church to recognize and remember its true identity: the church is nothing less than a community of end-time prophets called and empow-

---

come" (Matt. 24:14). Cf. Denzil R. Miller, *The Kingdom and the Power: A Pentecostal Interpretation* (Springfield, MO: AIA Publications, 2009).

[69] Roger Cotton, "Numbers 11 and Doing a Pentecostal, Biblical Theology of Church Leadership" (Springfield, MO: Assemblies of God Theological Seminary, PDF: 2http://www.agts.edu/faculty/faculty_publications/articles/cotton_numbers_11.html001), accessed Nov. 20, 2013.

[70] Roger Stronstad, *The Prophethood of All Believers: A Study in Luke's Charismatic Theology* (Cleveland, TN: CPT Press, 2010).

ered to bear bold witness for Jesus."[71] He continues, "For Pentecostals, then, tongues serves as a sign that the calling and power of the apostolic church are valid for contemporary believers."[72]

3. Tongues signify to the unbeliever that God is present and actively working among His people. Tongues also serve as a sign to the unbeliever. Writing to the church in Corinth Paul reminded them that "tongues are a sign ... for unbelievers" (1 Cor. 14:22). Luke develops this idea in his Pentecost narrative by telling how the gathered crowd, upon hearing the Spirit-inspired words of the 120, "were amazed and astonished, saying, 'Are not all these who are speaking Galileans? And how is it that we hear, each of us in his own native language?'" (Acts 2:7-8).

In this manner Luke presents speaking in tongues as one of those miraculous "signs and wonders"[73] which compelled people to listen to and believe the gospel. In many Majority World contexts unbelievers observing believers speaking in tongues can serve as a wonder every bit as much as seeing a healing take place—even if the tongue is not understood by the hearer as it was on the Day of Pentecost. Some, citing Paul's admonitions to the Corinthian church in 1 Corinthians 14, insist that all tongues speaking must be done in private, or they must always be interpreted. Unfortunately, in their rigid insistence

---

[71] Robert P. Menzies, *Pentecost: This Is Our Story* (Springfield, MO: Gospel Publishing House, 2013), 68.

[72] Ibid.

[73] "Signs and wonders" is a favorite phrase of Luke in Acts (cf. 2:22; 2:43; 3:10; 4:30; 5:12; 6:8; 7:36; 8:6, 13; 14:3).

on a Pauline, Corinthian-specific application of tongues, they have missed this powerful missional application of the practice.

Two common mistakes are made concerning speaking in tongues. First, there are those who emphasize speaking in tongues with no reference to the missional implications of the practice. Then, there are those who accentuate missions while ignoring the practice of speaking in tongues altogether. In Acts, however, Luke marries the two. For Luke, speaking in tongues is a missionary sign to the believer that he or she has been empowered to proclaim the gospel to the lost. It is further a sign to the believing community that they are a last-days Spirit-empowered missionary community, and to the unbeliever that God is manifestly present and speaking through His people. In the next two chapters I will discuss two more ways Luke presents speaking in tongues in the book of Acts: tongues as a prophetic release and tongues as an integral part of the empowering process.

– CHAPTER 5 –

LUKE'S MISSIONAL PRESENTATION OF TONGUES

PART 3:
TONGUES AS A PROPHETIC RELEASE

ACTS 2:4, 14, 16-17

*And they were all filled with the Holy Spirit
and began to speak in other tongues
as the Spirit gave them utterance.
... [then] Peter, standing with the eleven,
lifted up his voice and addressed them: ...
"This is what was uttered through the prophet Joel ...
'I will pour out my Spirit on all flesh, and your
sons and your daughters shall prophesy."*

ACTS 10:46

*For they were hearing them speaking in tongues
and extolling God.*

ACTS 19:6

And when Paul had laid his hands on them,
the Holy Spirit came on them, and they began
speaking in tongues and prophesying.

In Chapters 3 and 4 we began our discussion of Luke's presentation of tongues in the book of Acts. In these chapters we saw how he presented speaking in tongues as both a confirmatory evidence and as a missional sign. As a confirmatory evidence speaking in tongues affirms or verifies that one has indeed been empowered by the Holy Spirit as promised by Jesus in Acts 1:8 (cf. 10:44-47). As a missional sign it points to the greater meaning, or missional purpose of the experience it accompanies, that is, the baptism in the Holy Spirit as promised by Jesus and as received by the disciples on the Day of Pentecost (1:4-8; 2:4-11). In this chapter we will look at yet another way that Luke presents speaking in tongues in Acts, that is, tongues as a *prophetic release.*

Reexamining the Lukan Pattern

It is not without significance that in Acts Luke invariably couples speaking in tongues with prophetic proclamation of the gospel in the common language. This literary pattern is often overlooked when reading the three Lukan accounts of speaking in tongues (2:4; 10:46; 19:6). Pentecostal scholars have traditionally pointed to the Lukan pattern of Spirit baptism immediately followed by speaking in tongues. However, they have largely overlooked the equally significant pattern of Spirit-inspired speaking in tongues immediately followed by Spirit-inspired speech in the vernacular. This omission has regrettably caused many to miss the profound missional significance that Luke places on speaking in tongues in Acts. I have charted these two patterns in Figures 1 and 2 below.

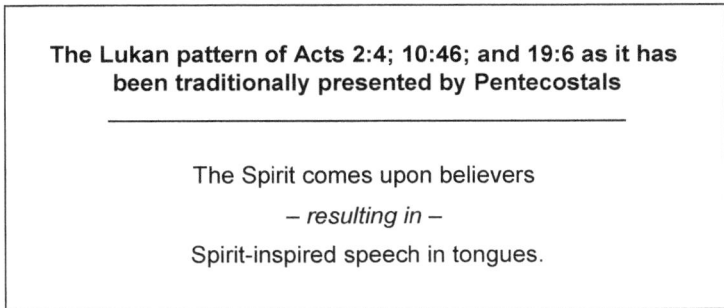

Figure 1

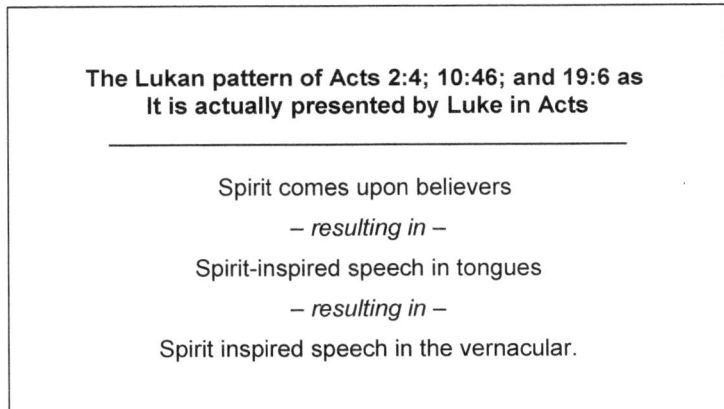

Figure 2

Luke thus never presents speaking in tongues as an end in itself, but rather as a means to an even greater end, that is, Spirit-inspired, prophetic proclamation of the gospel. This pattern accords well with Jesus' promise in Acts 1:8: "But you will receive power when the Holy Spirit has come upon you *and* you will be my witnesses." It is a motif that Luke did not want his readers to miss.

Tongues as a "heavenly spark"

It appears then that, according to Luke, one principal function of speaking in tongues is to facilitate an inner transformation of the heart—a sort of "heavenly spark"—that ignites the newly-Spirit-baptized disciple's spirit and releases his or her tongue to effectively declare the gospel to the lost in the common language.[74] Note how this prophetic release occurs in all three instances where speaking in tongues is mentioned in Acts:

- At Pentecost the 120 spoke in tongues as the Spirit enabled them *and then* Peter stood and proclaimed the gospel in the power of the Spirit (2:4; 14-40).
- At Caesarea the Gentile believers spoke in tongues *and then* extolled God (10:46).
- At Ephesus the twelve disciples spoke in tongues *and then* prophesied (19:6).

In each instance the disciple's reception of the Spirit accompanied by speaking in tongues engendered a subsequent prophetic release enabling the receivers to effectively speak the word of the Lord in the vernacular. Let's look more closely at each of the three recorded incidences in Acts where the recipients

---

[74] This possibly explains the significance of the "tongues as of fire" that appeared over the heads of the 120 disciples on the Day of Pentecost (Acts 2:3), and explains why Luke referred to them as *tongues* of fire rather than simply *flames* of fire.

spoke in tongues:

Prophetic Release at Pentecost

Immediately following the outpouring of the Spirit on the Day of Pentecost, accompanied by the disciples' speaking in unlearned, Spirit-enabled Gentile languages, Peter stood and boldly proclaimed Christ to the gathered multitude in the local vernacular.[75] As I have already noted, in both instances Peter was speaking as a Spirit-inspired prophet as foretold by the prophet Joel (2:28-29; cf. Acts 2:17-18). Judging from Luke's parallel phrasing in Chapter 2 (vv. 4 and 14), it appears that he intended for his readers to understand that Peter's speech in the common language was prompted and inspired by the Spirit just as was his earlier utterance in tongues.

Stanley Horton and others have perceptively noted how Luke uses the same Greek word *(apophtheggomai)* to describe both the 120's speaking in tongues in 2:4 as he does to describe Peter's subsequent proclamation of the gospel in the common language in verse 14, a detail that Luke's original Greek readers would have easily picked up on. The word means to speak out, or more literally, to "utter forth."[76] Following his Spirit-inspired uttering forth in an unlearned Gentile tongue, Peter, under the same pneumatic inspiration, stands and utters forth in the vernacular, declaring Christ to the gathered throng. It is quite probable that the other 119 newly Spirit-empowered

---

[75] The language spoken by Peter in his Pentecost sermon was most likely Aramaic, the common language spoken in Palestine during the first century.

[76] Thus the translation, "as the Spirit gave the utterance" in more literal translations such as the NKJV, ESV, RSV, and NASB.

disciples did the same in various venues and contexts throughout the city on that day and the days following, for Luke notes how "the Lord added to their number day by day those who were being saved" (v. 47).

Additionally, in his Pentecost address, by quoting from the prophet Joel Peter specifically identifies the disciples' speaking in tongues as prophetic utterance:

> But this *[speaking in tongues as the Spirit gives utterance that you have just witnessed]* is what was uttered through the prophet Joel: "And in the last days it shall be, God declares, that I will pour out my Spirit on all flesh, and *your sons and your daughters shall prophesy,* and your young men shall see visions, and your old men shall dream dreams; even on my male servants and female servants in those days I will pour out my Spirit, *and they shall prophesy."* (Acts 2:16-18, emphasis added)

By quoting Joel's prophecy Peter is saying to his listeners that these Spirit-inspired words they were hearing, first in tongues and now in their common dialect, are a direct fulfillment of Joel's prediction that in the last days of time all of God's people would be enabled to speak as Spirit-inspired prophets.

One mistake often made by New Testament scholars is to try to define prophecy as portrayed by Luke in Acts using Pauline categories. In his epistles Paul clearly distinguishes between the gift of tongues and the gift of prophecy. According to him, while both are Spirit-enabled, the first is spoken in a language unknown to the speaker while the second is spoken in a known language (1 Cor. 14:2-3).

What is not so generally understood is that Luke's presentation of tongues is not so nuanced as is Paul's. For him *all* Spirit-inspired speech is prophecy, whether it be in the vernacular or in tongues. In Luke's view, what makes speech prophetic is that it is inspired by the Spirit of God. Therefore, in Acts prophecy takes a number of forms including Spirit-inspired tongues (2:4; 10:46; 19:6), Spirit-prompted exhortation (13:2), and Spirit-revealed foretelling of future events (11:28; 21:10-11). The most common form of prophetic speech in Acts, however, is Spirit-empowered proclamation of the gospel to the lost. This kind of prophecy occurs in Acts in the following places:

- Peter at Pentecost (2:14-40)
- Peter at the Beautiful Gate (3:11-26; cf. 3:6 and 4:8)
- Peter and John before the Sanhedrin (4:8-12)
- The apostles in Jerusalem (4:31-33)
- Peter and John before the Sanhedrin again (5:29-32)
- Stephen (7:2-53, cf. 6:5-10, 15; 7:55)
- The scattered disciples (8:4)
- Philip in Samaria (8:5-6; 12-13,cf. 6:3, 5)
- Saul in Damascus (9:17-20; 22)
- Peter in Caesarea (10:34-44; 11:15)
- The scattered disciples in Antioch (11:20-21)
- Paul and Barnabas in Cyprus (13:4-5)
- Paul in Pisidian Antioch (13:16-52. Note v. 52)
- Paul in Iconium (14:1-3)
- Paul in Lystra (14:15-18. Note vv. 8-10)
- Paul in Thessalonica (17:1-4: cf. 1 Thess. 1:5-6)
- Paul in Corinth (18:4-5, 9; cf. 1 Cor. 2:4-5; 2 Cor. 12:12)
- Paul in Ephesus (19:8; cf. v. 6).

In each of the above instances Luke either explicitly states or strong implies by the context that these proclaimers of the gospel were speaking by the Spirit. Thus, in Lukan under standing, they were prophesying. In his exegetical commentary on Acts, Craig S. Keener makes a similar observation:

But prophecy, or inspired speech, in the most general sense is proclamation of the "word of the Lord," which in Acts includes the inspired gospel (e.g., 8:25; 12:24; 13:49). The heart of this calling, as defined in 1:8 is "witness" to all nations; that is, all the forms of inspired speech activity reflect or evoke the central commission of proclaiming God's central message of salvation in Christ, ... Inspired speech in other languages (2:4) offers a particularly apt illustration of the Spirit's empowerment to cross-cultural barriers in articulating this testimony, and the Diaspora Jews from a range of nations (2:1-11) prefigure the fulfillment of the mission to come.[77]

Prophetic Release in Caesarea

A prophetic release also occurred when the Holy Spirit fell on the Gentile believers gathered at the household of Cornelius in Caesarea. Luke states that on that occasion "the believers from among the circumcised who had come with Peter were amazed, because the gift of the Holy Spirit was poured out even on the Gentiles. For they were hearing them speaking in tongues *and extolling God"* (10:45-46, emphasis added). So, just as had happened to Peter at Pentecost, the infusion of the Spirit accompanied by Spirit-inspired speech in tongues produced in these Gentile receivers in Caesarea an inner release enabling them to also speak by the Spirit in the vernacular. As he did at Pentecost Luke again connects speaking in tongues with prophetic utterance in the common language.

The phrase "extolling God" in verse 46 lends itself to more than one interpretation. It is popularly understood to be de-

---

[77] Keener, Craig S., *Acts: An Exegetical Commentary, Volume 1, Introduction and 1:1–2:47* (Grand Rapids, MI: Baker Academic, 2012), 782.

scribing an elevated degree of praise and worship experienced by the Caesarean disciples once they had been filled with the Spirit. A more thoughtful examination of the text, however, reveals that the Gentiles' extolling God in Caesarea was more likely Spirit-inspired proclamation of the gospel as happened with Peter at Pentecost. As we have discussed earlier, this outpouring of the Spirit in Caesarea is, as on the Day of Pentecost, a direct fulfillment of the promise of Jesus in Acts 1:8: "You will receive power when the Holy Spirit has come upon you and you will be my witnesses ..." (cf. Acts 11:15-16). This is, I believe, what happened to those Gentiles who had gathered at Cornelius' residence that day: they spoke in tongues, and then, under the same inspiration of the Spirit, proclaimed the greatness of God to all who listen.

There are, after all, two ways a person may extol, or magnify, God. One can magnify Him by speaking directly to Him, telling Him of His greatness and praising Him for His mighty works. This is worship. Another way one can magnify God is by proclaiming His greatness to others. Either way God is exalted, and His name is magnified. It is more probable that the newly Spirit-baptized Gentiles in Caesarea exalted God in the second way.

An examination of the Greek word translated "extolling" in verse 46 *(megaloono)* seems to confirm this interpretation.[78] As I have previously discussed in *Empowered for Global Mission,* in each of the four other instances where Luke uses this word in Luke-Acts, he uses it to describe proclamation

---

[78] The word *megaloono* is variously translated "magnify" (KJV, NKJV), "extolling" (ESV, RSV), "praising" (NIV), and "exalting" (NASB).

directed at people rather than praise directed toward God.[79]
Here in Caesarea we have an example of what could be termed
"proclamational praise," that is, speaking the glories of God to
those who will listen. In his first epistle, Peter spoke of this
kind of praise:

> But you are a chosen generation, a royal priesthood, a holy
> nation, His own special people, that you may *proclaim the
> praises of Him who called you* out of darkness into His
> marvelous light. (1 Pet. 2:9, NKJV; emphasis added; cf.
> Psa. 51:15; 89:1).

The clearest example in the writings of Luke of his use of
megaloono to depict proclamational praise is found in Mary's
Magnificat. Listen closely to her words, and notice how she
directs her praise for God, not directly at Him but at others (to
help us see the direction of Mary's praise, I have italicized all
of the pronouns Mary uses to refer to God):

> And Mary said, "My soul magnifies (*megaloono*) the
> Lord, and my spirit rejoices in God my Savior,
> for *he* has looked on the humble estate of *his*
> servant.
> For behold, from now on all generations will call me
> blessed; for *he* who is mighty has done great things

---

[79] Denzil R. Miller, *Empowered for Global Mission*
(Springfield, MO: Life Publishers, 2005), 190-195. The other four
instances where Luke uses *megaloono* are Luke 1:46-47, Luke
1:58, Acts 5:13, and Acts 19:7. In *Empowered* I state, "Since in
every other case where Luke uses the word, or one of its
derivatives, he uses it in the sense of speaking praise words *about*
someone (either God or man) rather than *to* someone, it is
reasonable to conclude that *megaloono* in 10:46 could also be
describing the disciples' proclamation of God's greatness to
others" (193).

for me, and holy is *his* name.
And *his* mercy is for those who fear *him* from
    generation to generation.
He has shown strength with *his* arm;
    he has scattered the proud in the thoughts of their
    hearts; *he* has brought down the mighty from their
    thrones and exalted those of humble estate;
    he has filled the hungry with good things,
    and the rich *he* has sent away empty.
He has helped *his* servant Israel,
    in remembrance of *his* mercy, as *he* spoke to our
    fathers, to Abraham and to *his* offspring forever."
    (Luke 1:46-55, emphases added)

Note the similarities between this passage in Luke's gospel and the passage in Acts 10. Both Mary and the Gentile believers in Caesarea spoke by inspiration of the Holy Spirit,[80] and in both instances Luke uses the word *megaloono* to describe their speaking (compare Luke 1:46 with Acts 10:46). Note further how Mary's words of praise are directed, not toward God as one would in worship, but toward others as one would in proclamation. In her song of praise she never refers to God in the second person using the pronoun *you*. She does, however, mention Him 16 times in the third person using the pronouns *he* and *his*.[81] Nonetheless, Mary is indeed praising God by

---

[80] Cf. Luke 1:35; 41, 47; 10:44, 47. See James B. Shelton, "Was Mary Filled with the Spirit?" in *Mighty in Word and Deed: The Role of the Holy Spirit in Luke-Acts* (Peabody, MS: Hendrickson Publishers, 1991, 20-21, 31). See also Robert P. Menzies, *Empowered for Witness: The Spirit in Luke-Acts* (Sheffield, ENG: Sheffield Academic Press, 2001, 114-115).

[81] Another Lukan example of proclamational praise can be found in the prophetess Anna's declaration in Luke 2:38: "And coming up at that very hour she began to give thanks to God and to speak of him to all ..." Note how she simultaneously gave

declaring His greatness to others. It is likely that this is what occurred when the Spirit fell on the Gentiles at Cornelius' household: they spoke in tongues and extolled God, that is, they declared His magnificence to others.

This insight is important because, as I have already pointed out, the Gentiles' reception of the Spirit in Caesarea is a fulfillment of Jesus' missional promise in Acts 1:8, and it emphasizes the proclamational and missional importance of Spirit baptism. It further reminds us that we have not fully praised God as we should until we have declared His greatness to others!

Whether one interprets the word *extolling* in 10:46 as proclamation or worship, one fact remains; their extolling God is Spirit-inspired and follows as a direct consequence of the Gentile disciples' being filled with the Spirit *and* speaking in tongues. As happened at Pentecost (and as we will soon see, as will happen in Ephesus) their speaking in tongues in Caesarea sparked a prophetic release enabling them to magnify God more effectually in their own language.

Prophetic Release in Ephesus

A third prophetic release occurred in the lives of the twelve Ephesian disciples: "When the Holy Spirit came on them, and they began speaking in tongues *and* prophesying" (Acts 19:6, emphasis added). As in Jerusalem where Peter spoke in tongues *and then* proclaimed the gospel in the power of the Holy Spirit, and in Caesarea where the Gentile believers spoken in tongues *and then* magnified God, now the twelve disciples in Ephesus speak in tongues *and then* begin to prophesy. And, as in the

---

thanks to God and spoke of Him to others.

previous two instances, the prophetic speech in the vernacular is shown to be direct consequence of their being filled with the Spirit and speaking in tongues.

At this juncture, an important question must be answered: What was the nature of the twelve disciples' prophesying in verse 6? As stated above, we would err if we defined prophesying in this passage (or for that matter anywhere throughout Luke-Acts) by using the Pauline categories. Neither must we forget the context and purpose out of which each author wrote. Paul's context, as you will remember, is the church gathered in worship, and his purpose in writing was to bring the church back into Christian unity. On the other hand, Luke's context is the church scattered in mission, and his purpose in writing to motivate the church to move forward in Spirit-empowered evangelism and missions.

It is out of this second context that Luke writes, "When Paul had laid his hands on them, the Holy Spirit came on them, and they began speaking in tongues and prophesying." It therefore seems unlikely that their prophesying was the kind Paul describes in 1 Corinthians whose purpose was to build up, encourage, and console other believers (14:3). One can hardly imagine these twelve men standing around and one-by-one speaking personal prophecies over one another (as I once saw a group of "prophets" do on Christian television). Such a vision in no way comports with the missionary theme and thrust of Luke's narrative, nor does it fit the immediate context of Paul's missionary ministry in Ephesus. Their prophecy is best understood in the Lukan sense of Spirit-empowered witness. Thus, just as at Pentecost the 120 were filled with the Spirit, spoke in tongues, and proclaimed Christ to the lost, and in Caesarea the Gentile believers spoke in tongues and exalted

God through proclamational praise, now in Ephesus the twelve disciples are filled with the Spirit, speak in tongues, and prophetically proclaim Christ to the lost.

Luke goes on to tell us how this outpouring of the Spirit in Ephesus, accompanied by Spirit-anointed speech in tongues and in the vernacular, resulted in powerful evangelistic outreach in Ephesus and throughout the entire Roman province of Asia. Once the twelve had been empowered by the Spirit, Paul immediately took them and entered into the Jewish synagogue proclaiming the kingdom of God. This evangelistic outreach soon extended to all of the region, so that after only two years "all the residents of Asia heard the word of the Lord, both Jews and Greeks" (v. 10).[82] In reading this account we must not miss the direct connection that Luke makes between the twelve disciples' being filled with the Spirit, their speaking in tongues and prophesying, and the powerful missionary outreach that resulted.

It is also significant that such Spirit-anointed, prophetic proclamation of the Kingdom is in accordance with the pattern first established by Jesus and particularly highlighted by Luke throughout his corpus. Of all the evangelists, only he tells us that Jesus was Himself anointed by the Spirit "*to proclaim* good news to the poor ... *to proclaim* liberty to the captives and recovering of sight to the blind, to set at liberty those who are oppressed, *to proclaim* the year of the Lord's favor" (Luke

---

[82] Luke uses Paul's ministry in Asia to illustrate and summarize the missionary strategy he used throughout his missionary career. I call this strategy the "New Testament Strategy of the Spirit." I discuss this strategy at length in my book, *Empowered for Global Mission* (235-242). I also discuss it in my book *The Spirit of God in Mission: A Vocational Commentary on the Book of Acts* (Springfield, MO: PneumaLife Publications, 2013, 194-197).

4:18-19, emphasis added; cf. Isa. 61:1-2). In Acts the disciples' Spirit-anointed proclamation was both public and private (Acts 20:20) and resulted in, among other things astonishment at the word (2:12: 4:13; 6:7; 9:21; 13:12), deep inner conviction (2:37; 6:10; 16:14), resistance to the gospel (4:1; 5:33; 7:54; 14:45: 17:5, 32; 18:6), and most notably, faith in Christ (4:4, 32; 6:7; 8:12; 11:21; 14:48;16:34; 17:34).

As with the other two instances in Acts, the outpouring of the Spirit in Ephesus is a fulfillment of Jesus' promise in Acts 1:8. And, as I mentioned in Chapter 3, Luke narratively connects these three instances to Jesus' final promise by using the same "coming on" metaphor in each instance to describe the Spirit's work in the lives of the disciples:

- Acts 1:8   "But you will receive power when the Holy Spirit *has come upon* you"

- Acts 2:3   "tongues as of fire ... *rested on* each one of them"
- Acts 10:44 "the Holy Spirit *fell on* all who heard the word"
- Acts 19:6   "the Holy Spirit *came on* them."

Understanding how Luke linguistically connects these three incidences to His promise of power in Acts 1:8 helps us to better understand what is happening in each instance. As Jesus had prophesied, the Spirit "came upon" each group to empower them as His witnesses, and each time He came upon them the result was the same, Spirit-inspired speech both in tongues and in the vernacular. On each occasion that Spirit-inspired speech had (and still has) profound missional implications. May God forgive us if we have ignored or trivialized those implications.

In Acts Luke presents Spirit baptism as a powerful missions oriented experience accompanied by Spirit-inspired prophetic speech in both unlearned and learned languages. This twofold dynamic speaks to the prophetic and missional nature of the gift, and both kinds of Spirit-inspired speech appear to be essential components of one's being fully empowered by the Spirit as promise by Jesus in Acts 1:8. In other words, speaking in tongues, if not followed by prophetic proclamation, loses much of its significance; and missional proclamation without a prior prophetic release in tongues loses much of its divine power and efficacy.

In recent years I have sought to apply this missional understanding concerning speaking in tongues to my ministry of praying with believers to be filled with the Spirit—and thus empowered by Him to reach the lost for Christ. One way I have done this is by instructing those who come to be filled to "expect to speak by the Spirit *two ways!*" First, they should expect to be enabled and prompted by the Spirit within to speak in tongues. Then, from that moment on, they should expect to be enabled and prompted by the Spirit, not only to speak in tongues, but to speak to their lost friends about Jesus. Numerous testimonies have proven the effectiveness of this practice. It is a practical model that, I believe, captures the true spirit and purpose of Luke's teaching on speaking in tongues in Acts and echos Jesus' last word to His church: "But you will receive power when the Holy Spirit has come upon you, *and* you will be my witnesses" (Acts 1:8).

While Classical Pentecostals have done well in holding to their doctrine of "subsequence," meaning Spirit baptism is an experience subsequent to and separate from the new birth, the time is ripe for them to emphasize a second kind of subsequence, that is, Spirit-enabled witness subsequent to, yet intimately connected with, Spirit-inspired speaking in tongues. In the next chapter I will pursue this thought further. I will discuss how Luke presents tongues as an enabling element, or part and parcel of the empowering event of Spirit baptism.

– CHAPTER 6 –

LUKE'S MISSIONAL PRESENTATION OF TONGUES

PART 4:
TONGUES AS AN EMPOWERING ELEMENT

ACTS 1:8; 2:4

But you will receive power
when the Holy Spirit has come upon you...
And they were all filled with the Holy Spirit
and began to speak in other tongues
as the Spirit gave them the utterance.

1 CORINTHIANS 14:4:

The one who speaks in a tongue builds up himself.

Not only does Luke present tongues as a confirmatory evidence, a missional sign, and a prophetic release, he further presents them as an *enabling element*. For him they were neither peripheral nor incidental to the experience of Spirit baptism, as they seem to be for so many Pentecostals today. For Luke tongues were part and parcel of the empowering experience.

We actually began this chapter's discussion in the last chapter where we discussed tongues as a prophetic release. To fully understand Luke's perspective concerning the role of speaking in tongues in Spirit-empowered ministry, we will need expand on this idea a bit more. While this perspective of Luke's is not as openly apparent in Acts as the previous three, it is, nevertheless, clearly indicated in the book.

Scott T. Bottoms refers to this enabling function of tongues as "incarnational tongues," contending that in Acts Luke presents tongues as a means by which the missionary Spirit incarnates Himself in God's people to empower them as Christ's missionary witnesses. According to Bottoms, "Luke not only saw tongues as evidence of the Spirit's empowerment, but as an integral part of the same."[83] Combining Luke's teaching on the Spirit's empowering believers for witness (Acts 1:8, 2:4, et al.) with Paul's teaching that "the one who speaks in a tongue builds up himself" (1 Cor. 14:4), Bottoms contends that one can logically infer that one primary way the Spirit builds up the one who speaks in tongues is by inspiring and empowering them to witness for Christ. According to Bottoms, then, Paul's edificational view of tongues includes the missional empowering Jesus promised in Acts 1:8 and received by the disciples in 2:4. Bottoms applies his teaching:

---

[83] Scott T. Bottoms, "Restoring the Centrality of the Spirit's Empowerment for Carrying out the Great Commission: A Course to Equip Christians at Journey Church in the Process of Evangelism" (D.Min. project, Assemblies of God Theological Seminary, 2011), 39.

The practice becomes especially important at this point. If tongues is an actual part of the empowerment process, and not just a sign of the same, then tongues becomes a necessary ingredient in missional empowerment.... The believer needs to speak in tongues precisely because tongues is itself part of the empowering work of the Spirit, and therefore a vital key to effective evangelism.[84]

Tongues thus emerges as an integral part of the empowering process. Believing that the Classical Pentecostal's sometimes narrow focus on tongues as the "initial physical evidence" of Spirit baptism is an inadequate understanding of Luke's missional view of the practice, Bottoms continues.

Luke's goal in emphasizing tongues was not simply to signify the moment a believer is baptized in the Spirit, but as an incarnational sign declaring that the believer's life has been imbued with divine power and purpose. The disciple is now ready for Spirit-empowered ministry and has the access to the empowerment that prayer in tongues brings to an otherwise inconsequential human life.[85]

If Bottoms' insights are valid, and I believe that they are, the practice of speaking in tongues is elevated from the sometimes narcissistic tongues-as-a-means-of-personal-blessing construct held by many Pentecostals and Charismatic Christians today. Tongues are necessary, not simply because they evidence one's reception of the Spirit, but because they are part and parcel of the empowering process itself.

This missional empowering takes place, not only when one is first baptized in the Holy Spirit signified by speaking in

---

[84] Ibid, 50.

[85] Ibid, 60.

tongues, it occurs again and again each time the Spirit-filled believer prays in the Spirit. After speaking of the edificational benefit of tongues (1 Cor 14:4), Paul declares, "I thank God that I speak in tongues more than you all" (v. 18). Paul presents prayer in tongues as an ongoing and beneficial practice for Christians. This idea is also inferred in Romans 8 where he encourages believers to intercede in the Spirit "with groans too deep for words" (v. 26).

While in Acts Luke does not directly speak of ongoing prayer in tongues, the idea is implied by his use of the transitive verb "began" (Gk: *archomai*) in Acts 2:4: "They... *began* to speak in other tongues as the Spirit gave them utterance." It is not unreasonable to assume that in using this word Luke was inferring that the disciples' speaking in tongues at Pentecost was merely the first of many times they would be filled with the Spirit and speak in tongues as the Spirit enabled them. When we combine this idea with Paul's teaching concerning a believer's praying often in the Spirit, this is not an unreasonable assumption.

This idea of continued prayer in the Spirit is also implied in Luke's account of Jesus' teaching on how His disciples may be filled with—and remain full of— the Spirit (Luke 11:1-13). In this passage Jesus encourages His disciples, to boldly "ask," "seek," and "knock" because "the heavenly Father [will] give the Holy Spirit to those who ask him!" (vv. 9, 13). Pentecostal scholar Stanley Horton has pointed out how a literal reading of Jesus words in verses 9-10 would proceed something like this:

Ask [keep asking], and it shall be given you; seek [keep on seeking], and ye shall find; knock [keep knocking], and it shall be opened unto you. For every one that asketh [keeps on asking, who is an 'asker'] receiveth [keeps on receiving]; and he that seeketh [who keeps on seeking, who is a 'seeker'] findeth [keeps on finding]; and to him that knocketh [who makes it his practice to knock on doors] it shall be opened.[86]

It therefore follows that if, as I am suggesting, speaking in tongues is an integral part of the empowering process, then regular prayer in the Spirit would also help to enable the following Spirit-enabled practices found in Acts:

- Insight into the meaning and implications of Scripture (2:17-21)
- Ability to speak with greater confidence and authority (2:41; 4:31-33)
- Increased zeal to speak out on Christ's behalf (2:12ff, 41, 47; 4:20; 11:12)
- Boldness to speak in the face of opposition (4:31; 5:22; 18:9)
- Power to confront and defeat demonic powers (16:16-18; 19:15-16)
- Greater capacity to be used in the manifestation of spiritual gifts (2:43;6:8; 8:6; 14:3)
- Confidence to persevere in times of stress and discouragement (Acts 18:9)
- Guidance to the field of services (8:29; 10:19; 16:7-10).

If these things be true, then the practice of speaking in tongues is elevated from the sometimes self-centered practice that many contemporary Pentecostal and Charismatic Christians have made it, to an essential ongoing enabling practice as disciples daily prepare themselves to go into their worlds to

---

[86] Stanley Horton, *What the Bible Says About the Holy Spirit* (Springfield, MO: Gospel Publishing House, 1989), 104.

spread the message of Christ's love. In this context, prayer in tongues is no longer an optional practice for some, but an essential daily discipline for all who name the name of Christ. How foolish we would be to neglect the powerful missional practice of daily prayer in the Spirit.

Practical Application: Witnessing in the Spirit

There is yet another way that speaking in tongues prepares us for prophetic witness, or the kind of Spirit-empowered, Spirit-directed witness we see on display in the book of Acts. I call this kind of witnessing "witnessing in (or by) the Spirit." In this kind of witness, as I briefly mentioned in Chapters 2 and 5, the Spirit Himself speaks through the Spirit-anointed disciple announcing the message of Christ to all will hear. It is the kind of speech that Jesus described as being "full of the Spirit and life" (John 6:63, TNIV).[87] This kind of Spirit-energized witness occurred at Pentecost when the Spirit Himself spoke to the crowds, first through the 120, and then through Peter's Spirit-inspired sermon (Acts 2:5-7; 14-40). It resulted in sinners being "cut to the heart" and crying out "what shall we do?" (v. 37).[88] The same kind of witness occurred on subsequent occasions in Act (4:8; 31; 13:9-10).

Speaking in tongues uniquely prepares one for this sort of prophetic witness. Through speaking in tongues, the Spirit-filled disciple vicariously "practices" the kind of faith-filled

---

[87] The New Testament: Today's New International Version (Grand Rapids, MI: Zondervan, 2002).

[88] Contrast this kind of witness with the pedestrian way that most witnessing is done today where sincere but uninspired believers seek to influence people to Christ through humanly engendered words spoken out of their own hearts and intellects.

yielding to the Spirit and Spirit-prompted speech essential to witness in the Spirit. The way one responds to the Spirit when he or she is prompted by the Spirit to speak in tongues is the same as when he or she is prompted by the Spirit to speak "all the words of this life" in the common language to the lost. Allow me to elaborate.

Over the past two decades I have been privileged to pray with thousands of sincere seekers and marvel as God graciously filled them with His Spirit accompanied by the miracle of speaking in tongues. I never cease to be awed by this wonderful happening. Throughout the years I have tried to learn from these experiences by comparing their experience with my own and with the teachings of Scripture. In doing this I have observed an often unconscious, yet consistent process that occurs when believers are filled with the Spirit.

The process begins when in faith the seeker asks God for the Spirit, fully expecting Him to hear and answer his prayer (Luke 11:9-13; Mark 11:24). God then, according to His promise, responds to the seeker's request, and graciously pours His Spirit upon him (Luke 11:9). Once the seeker senses the Holy Spirit's presence upon him, he invites the Spirit to come in and fill him.[89] The seeker will again sense the Spirit's presence, this time deep within his own human spirit. He then yields to the Spirit's impulse, and allowing the Spirit's fulness to flow out "from his innermost being" (John 7: 38, NASB), he begins to speak out in faith, not knowing what he is going to

---

[89] When praying with seekers, I, at this point, often instruct them to pray this simple prayer: "In Jesus' name, I receive the Spirit" (cf. Luke 11:9-10), and to believe that, at that very moment, God is filling them with His Spirit (Mark 11:24). Sometimes it is helpful to encourage them to "breathe" in the Spirit (John 20:21), that is, to consciously and actively respond to the Spirit's coming in.

say but fully trusting God to supernaturally supply the words. Miraculously he begins to speak in an unlearned language (Acts 2:4) signifying that he has been empowered by the Spirit to speak on Christ's behalf (Acts 1:8). The words he speaks, however, do not come from his mind as in normal speech, but from deep within, from his spirit. As Paul testified, "For if I pray in a tongue, my spirit prays but my mind is unfruitful (1 Cor. 14:14).[90] Along with the speaking in tongues comes an inner compulsion to tell the lost about Christ. This profound spiritual activity should be the daily habit of every believer in Christ.

What is often missed is how closely the process of one's receiving the Spirit and speaking in tongues parallels the process of Spirit-directed witness in the vernacular, or as I have termed it, *witnessing in the Spirit.* The parallels are significant, the former naturally preparing the way for the latter. This is aptly demonstrated by Peter's example at Pentecost. First the Spirit came upon, filled, and empowered Peter and the other 119 waiting disciples. They then began to "utter forth" *(apophtheggomai)* in unlearned Gentile tongues as the Spirit enabled them. A few minutes later the Spirit came upon Peter a second time, and he "uttered forth" again, this time in the common language, declaring the message of the risen Christ to the gathered throng (vv. 14-40).

In like manner, when a believer today is filled with the Spirit accompanied by Spirit-inspired speech in an unlearned language, a number of spiritual dynamics occur. First, there comes into his heart an inner compulsion, not only to speak in

---

[90] Interestingly, the Good News Bible paraphrases this verse,"For if I pray in this way, my spirit prays indeed, but my mind has no part in it."

tongues, but to speak out in the vernacular telling others about Christ. If the recipient understands this dynamic, and is properly taught how to respond to it, he is now in a position to begin witnessing in the Spirit. Then, when at the appropriate time the Spirit prompts, he will understand better how to properly respond, and as with Peter at Pentecost, will begin to speak to the lost person "as the Spirit gives the utterance" (Acts 2:4, 14). The Spirit will once again come upon him, fill him, and prompt him to speak out in Spirit-inspired witness to the lost. Much like when he speaks in tongues, the Spirit-filled disciple will begin to speak, not knowing exactly what he is going to say, but trusting the Lord to give him the appropriate words.

Once they learn to witness by the Spirit's prompting, he or she can anticipate that the Spirit will set up "divine appointments" and direct them into these witnessing opportunities, just as He did for Philip (Acts 8:26-39), Peter (Acts 10:9-24), and others in Acts.

The chart on the next page helps us to see how the two processes of being filled with the Spirit accompanied by speaking in tongues and being "anointed" by the Spirit resulting in Spirit-directed witness parallel one another—the first being preparation for the second.

Figure 2 A Comparison: The Spiritual Dynamics of Receiving the Spirit and Witnessing in the Spirit	
Receiving the Holy Spirit	Witnessing in the Spirit
The seeker asks the Spirit to come upon him and fill him.	The witness asks the Spirit to anoint him and prepare him for witness.
God responds by pouring out His Spirit on the expectant seeker.	God responds by coming upon the Spirit-filled witness.
The seeker senses and responds to the Spirit's coming upon and filling him.	The witness senses and responds to the Spirit's coming upon and anointing him for witness.
The Spirit prompts the seeker to speak out in faith.	The Spirit prompts the witness to speak out in faith.
The seeker speaks out, not knowing what he will say, but fully trusting God for the words.	The witness speaks out, not knowing exactly what he will say, but fully trusting God for the words.
God miraculously supplies the words in an unknown tongue.	God miraculously supplies the words in the common language.

– CHAPTER 7 –

A TIME FOR REDISCOVERY

In this study we have discussed how early Pentecostal leaders embraced a bold and dynamic view of the empowering work of the Holy Spirit in the lives of believers. They believed that in these last days of time God was restoring to his church the same power and glory it had at the beginning. He was doing this in order to enable the church to evangelize the nations before the soon coming of Christ.

Missionary Tongues

At the center of this restorationist impulse was the expectation that God would baptize believers in the Holy Spirit accompanied by the same "Bible evidence" as was received by believers at Pentecost and in other places in the book of Acts, that is, recipients of the Spirit would speak in tongues as the Spirit gave them the utterance. They further believed that the tongues spoken would be actual living human languages as were promised by Jesus in His Great Commission and experienced by the disciples on the day of Pentecost (Mark 16:17; Acts 2:6-7). These supernaturally enabled missionaries would then be able to go quickly into all the world and preach the gospel without the time consuming need to study languages, thus hastening the return of Christ (Matt. 24:14 with 2 Pet. 3:12). They called this phenomenon "missionary tongues."

This theology was soon put to the test as these "new-tongued missionaries" were sent out from the Azusa Street Mission and other centers of Pentecostal revival. Upon arriving at their places of service on the foreign fields, however, the practice soon proved to be unworkable, and was quickly abandoned, along with the theology supporting it. Unfortunately, with the abandonment the concept of xenolalic missionary tongues came a concurrent loss of understanding concerning the missional nature of speaking in tongues in general. Nevertheless, while the early Pentecostals' bold experiment with missionary tongues was a failure, they were, I believe, right to place speaking in tongues into missiological categories.

However, even as the missionary tongues doctrine was being abandoned, the "Bible evidence" (or "initial physical evidence") teaching was being reaffirmed. Reconciling this Lukan emphasis of tongues as an evidence of Spirit baptism with the Pauline emphases of tongues as a congregational gift and a personal prayer language, Pentecostals formulated their commonly-held understanding concerning speaking in tongues, an understanding that has endured until today. Unfortunately, in the reformulating of their doctrine of tongues something valuable was lost. While Pentecostals held (at least in part) to the concept that the baptism in the Holy Spirit was itself a missionally empowering experience, they moved away from the early idea that the accompanying sign also had intrinsic missional implications. As the years passed, Luke's missional understanding of tongues was all but lost. This widespread lack of understanding has persisted until the present.

This lack of understanding, along with the countless episodes of misuse and abuse in Pentecostal and Charismatic congregations around the world, has tragically resulted in a devaluing of the practice in the eyes of many. Consequently, many once spiritually vibrant Pentecostal churches have been nominalized, and the gift of the Spirit is no longer embraced nor actively sought after in their midst. In the process the once cherished Pentecostal practice of speaking in tongues has been marginalized, and in many cases abandoned altogether.

Today, with the emergence of a new passion among Pentecostals to reach the world's unreached peoples and places before the soon coming of Christ, the time is ripe to revisit the book of Acts and rediscover Luke's compelling presentation of tongues. Our current era of ignorance concerning the missional nature of tongues, and the neglect engendered by that ignorance, must come to an end. It is high time for Pentecostals to rediscover the true nature and powerful missional implications of speaking in tongues as presented by Luke in the book of Acts.

Summary and insights

In this book I have sought to address this important issue. I have presented what I believe to be an accurate portrayal of Luke's missional view of tongues. In doing this I hope to begin a conversation among serious-minded, mission-oriented Pentecostal scholars. I further hope to challenge Pentecostal leaders to boldly reevaluate the current Pentecostal approach to speaking in tongues in light of these insights. Hopefully, out of this conversation will emerge a new commitment on the part of Pentecostal leaders to see believers baptized in the Holy Spirit, complete with the *normative missional sign*[91] of speaking in tongues as the Spirit gives utterance. In addition, I hope that committed Pentecostal believers will be encouraged to practice frequent personal prayer in the Spirit, not only as a personal prayer language, but as a daily means of empowerment for witness.

In this book I have suggested four ways Luke presents speaking in tongues in Acts. Each way grows naturally out of the context of his missional teaching on the Spirit, and each reflects his missio-pneumatic intent in writing Acts. I have suggested that in Acts Luke presents tongues as a *confirmatory evidence*, as a *missional sign*, as a *prophetic release*, and as an *empowering element*. To the degree that these insights are valid, they cumulatively demonstrate the vital importance of the practice to the fulfillment of God's mission in the world today.

Missional Implications

This fourfold Lukan understanding of tongues has potentially powerful missional implications for the Pentecostal church today, and could serve the movement in at least three significant ways: First, it could serve as a needed correction to

---

[91] In recent years there has risen among Pentecostal scholars and practitioners a discussion concerning the best phrase to use to describe the nature and purpose of speaking in tongues in Acts. Pentecostals have historically employed the phrases "initial evidence" or "initial physical evidence" to describe it. Other suggested phrases I have heard are that tongues are the "concomitant sign" or the "prophetic confirmation" that one has been baptized in the Holy Spirit. While personally I am not prepared to abandon the term "initial physical evidence" altogether, for a number of reasons I believe that the term "normative missional sign" more accurately describes Luke's presentation of tongues in Acts.

the sometimes self-centered and static (that is, non-missional) view many Pentecostals presently hold concerning the practice of speaking in tongues. In earlier chapters I have described the current, commonly-held theology concerning tongues in Acts as a "theology without feet," that is, a theology that does not move us into mission. However, as believers begin to understanding that speaking in tongues is God's confirming sign that they have been empowered by the Spirit to reach the lost, great confidence will come into their hearts along with motivation to begin actively witnessing for Christ. When they realize that speaking in tongues is part and parcel of the empowering process they will be encouraged to return again and again to their prayer closets and pray often in the Spirit in order that they might be ready when a witnessing opportunity presents itself.

Further, this new Lukan understanding of speaking in tongues carries with it the potential of significantly increasing the "value" of the practice in the minds of many sincere, yet disillusioned, Pentecostal believers. Unfortunately, these "reluctant Pentecostals" have repeatedly observed the gift of tongues misused and trivialized in their churches, and as a result, have lost confidence in the practice. However, when they come to realize the powerful missional implications of speaking in tongues as presented by Luke in Acts, and observe the experience's dramatic impact in the lives of others, they will be encouraged to seek the experience for themselves and to practice daily prayer in the Spirit.

Finally, if Luke's missional presentation of speaking in tongues was to become widely understood by Pentecostal preachers and teachers, it would help to catalyze effective life-changing preaching and teaching in their churches and ministerial training institutions. Leaders would begin to model the practice in their own lives and encourage others to be filled with the Spirit and to make prayer in the Spirit a daily practice in their lives.

A Final Word

As we seek to bring closure to the Great Commission and to bear witness to Christ "in Jerusalem, Judea and Samaria, and to the end of the earth," we must, as never before, go in the power of the Spirit. And if tongues are, as I have presented in this book, truly part and parcel of our receiving the Spirit's power, this truth becomes a compelling reason why all true missions-minded Pentecostals must contend for tongues as the normative missional sign of receiving the Holy Spirit.

While we must hold firm to this verificational function of tongues, we must expand our understanding of the experience. *Tongues are more than an evidence,* they are also a powerful missional sign, a dynamic prophetic release, and an integral enabling element to one's being empowered by the Spirit to proclaim the message of Christ to the ends of the earth before His imminent return.

WORKS CITED

Acts in Africa website. http//:www.actsinafrica.org. Accessed
    January 24, 2014.

Arrington, French L. "Hermeneutics, Historical Perspectives on
    Pentecostal and Charismatic." In *Dictionary of Pentecostal
    and Charismatic Movements,* edited by Stanley M. Burgess
    and Gary B McGee. Grand Rapids: Zondervan Publishers,
    1988.

Assemblies of God, USA. Statement of Fundamental Truths,
    Section 7, "Baptism in the Holy Spirit."

Bottoms, Scott T. "Restoring the Centrality of the Spirit's
    Empowerment for Carrying out the Great Commission: A
    Course to Equip Christians at Journey Church in the Process of
    Evangelism" (D.Min. project, Assemblies of God Theological
    Seminary, 2011).

Carson, D. A. *Showing the Spirit: A Theological Exposition
    of 1 Corinthians 12-14,* 6th printing. Grand Rapids, MI: Baker
    Book House, 2000.

Church of God, International, Cleveland, TN, USA. "Official
    Declaration of Faith."

Cotton, Roger. "Numbers 11 and Doing a Pentecostal, Biblical
    Theology of Church Leadership." Springfield, MO:
    Assemblies of God Theological Seminary, PDF: 2http://
    www.agts.edu/faculty/faculty_publications/articles/
    cotton_numbers_11.html001. Accessed November 20, 2013.

Cox, Harvey. *Fire from Heaven: The Rise of Pentecostal
    Spirituality and the Reshaping of Religion in the Twenty-first
    Century.* Cambridge, MA: Da Capo Press, 2001.

Crosby, Robert. "The Pentecostal Paradox: As the Global Chorus
    Grows, American Tongues Fall Silent." Patheos.com:
    http://www.patheos.com/Resources/Additional-Resources/
    Pentecostal-Paradox-Robert-Crosby-01-27-2012.html.
    Accessed Feb. 19, 2014.

Decade of Pentecost website. www.decadeofpentecost.org. Accessed Dec. 20 2013.

Dunn, James D. G. *Baptism in the Holy Spirit: A Re-examination of the New Testament Teaching on the Gift of the Spirit in Relation to Pentecostalism Today.* Philadelphia, PA: The Westminister Press, 1970.

Ervin, Howard M. *Conversion-Initiation and the Baptism in the Holy Spirit: A Critique of James D. G. Dunn.* Peabody, MA: Hendrickson Publishers, 1984.

Fee, Gordon D. and Douglas Stuart. *How to Read the Bible for All Its Worth: A Guide to Understanding the Bible.* Grand Rapids, MI: Zondervan, 2003.

Frodsham, Stanley. *With Signs Following.* Springfield, MO: Gospel Publishing House, 1946.

Goff, James R., Jr. *Fields White unto Harvest: Charles F. Parham and the Missionary Origins of Pentecostalism.* Fayetteville, AR: University of Arkansas Press, 1988.

_____. "Initial Tongues in the Theology of Charles Fox Parham." In *Evidential Tongues: Historical and Biblical Perspectives on the Pentecostal Doctrine of Spirit Baptism,* edited by Gary B. McGee. Peabody, MA: Hendrickson Publishers, 1991.

Graves, Robert W. "The Use of *gar* in Acts 10:46." In *Paraclete* 22, no. 2 (Spring 1988).

Horton, Stanley. *What the Bible Says About the Holy Spirit.* Springfield, MO: Gospel Publishing House, 1989.

Jacobsen, Douglas. *Thinking in the Spirit: Theologies of the Early Pentecostal Movement.* Bloomington, IN: Indiana University Press, 2003.

Kähler, Martin. *Schriften zur Christologie und Mission,* 1971, translated by David Bosch in *Transforming Mission: Paradigm Shifts in Theology of Mission.* Maryknoll, NY: Orbis Books, 1991.

Keener, Craig S. *Acts: An Exegetical Commentary, Vol. 1, Introduction and 1:1–2:47.* Grand Rapids, MI: Baker Academic, 2012.

_____. *Gift and Giver: The Holy Spirit for Today.* Grand Rapids, MI: Baker Academic, 2001.

Klein, William W., Craig L. Blomberg, and Robert L. Hubbard, Jr. *Introduction to Biblical Interpretation.* Nashville, TN: Word Publishing Group, 1993.

Kraft, Charles H. "A Third Wave Perspective on Pentecostal Missions." In *Called and Empowered: Global Mission in Pentecostal Perspective,* eds. Murray A. Dempster, Byron D. Klaus, and Douglas Petersen. Peabody, MA: Hendrickson Publishers, 1991.

Lederle, Henry. "Evidence and Movement." In *Initial Evidence Historical and Biblical Perspectives on the Pentecostal Doctrine of Spirit Baptism,* ed. Gary B. McGee. Peabody: MS: Hendrickson, 1991.

_____. *Theology with Spirit: The Future of the Pentecostal and Charismatic Movements in the 21st Century.* Tulsa, OK: Word and Spirit Press, 2010.

Macchia, Frank. "The Struggle for Global Witness: Shifting Paradigms in Pentecostal Theology." In *The Globalization of Pentecostalism: A Religion Made to Travel,* eds. Murray W. Dempster, Byron D. Klaus, and Douglas Petersen. Irvine, CA: Regnum Books, 1999.

_____. "Theology, Pentecostal." In *The New International Dictionary of Pentecostal and Charismatic Movements: Revised and Expanded Edition,* edited by Stanley M. Burgess. Grand Rapids, MI: Zondervan, 2002.

Marshall, I. Howard. *Luke Historian and Theologian.* Grand Rapids: Zondervan, 1970.

McGee, Gary B. "Missions, Overseas (North America)." In *Dictionary of Pentecostal and Charismatic Movements,* edited by Stanley M. Burgess and Gary B. McGee. Grand Rapids, MI: Regency Reference Library, Zondervan

Publishing House, 1988.

_____. "Early Pentecostal Hermeneutics: Tongues as Evidence in the Book of Acts." In *Evidential Tongues: Historical and Biblical Perspectives on the Pentecostal Doctrine of Spirit Baptism,* edited by Gary B. McGee. Peabody, MA: Hendrickson Publishers, 1991.

_____. "All for Jesus: The Revival Legacy of A.B. Simpson." In *Enrichment Journal*, http:/enrichmentjournal. ag.org/199903/ 068_tongues.cfm. Accessed Oct. 21, 2013.

Menzies, Robert P. *Empowered for Witness: The Spirit in Luke-Acts.* Sheffield, ENG: Sheffield Academic Press, Ltd, 2001.

_____. *Pentecost: This Is Our Story.* Springfield, MO: Gospel Publishing House, 2013.

Menzies, William W. and Robert P. Menzies. *Spirit and Power: Foundations of Pentecostal Experience.* Grand Rapids, MI: Zondervan, 2000.

Miller, Denzil R. *Empowered for Global Mission: A Missionary Look at the Book of Acts.* Springfield, MO: Life Publishers International, 2005.

_____. *From Azusa to Africa to the Nations.* Springfield, MO: Assemblies of God World Missions: Africa Office, 2005.

_____. *In Step with the Spirit: Studies in the Spirit-filled Walk.* Springfield, MO: AIA Publications, 2008.

_____. *The Kingdom and the Power: A Pentecostal Interpretation.* Springfield, MO: AIA Publications, 2009.

_____. *Implications of Lukan Pneumatology: Doctoral Study Guide,* 6th ed, reviewed by Roger Stronstad and James M. Thacker. Lome, Togo: Pan-Africa Theological Seminary, 2013.

Shelton, James B. *Mighty in Word in Deed: The Role of the Holy Spirit in Luke-Acts.* Peabody, MA: Hendrickson Publishers, 1991.

Spirit and Power: A 10-Country Survey of Pentecostals. Washington, D.C.: Pew Research Center, 2007.

Stott, John R. W. *Baptism and Fullness of the Holy Spirit.* Downers Grove, IL: Inter-Varsity Press, 1964.

Stronstad, Roger. *The Charismatic Theology of St. Luke.* Peabody, MA: Hendrickson Publishers, 1984.

_____. *The Prophethood of All Believers: A Study in Luke's Charismatic Theology.* Cleveland, TN: CPT Press, 2010.

_____. *Signs on the Earth Below: A Commentary on Acts 2:1-21.* Springfield, MO: Life Publishers International, 2003.

Studd, C. T. "Trumpet Calls to Britain's Sons." In *The Evangelisation of the World, a Missionary Band: A Record of Consecration, and an Appeal,* 3rd ed., edited by B Broomhall. London: Morgan and Scott, 1889. Cited by Gary B. McGee in "Shortcut to Language Preparation? Radical Evangelicals, Missions, and the Gift of Tongues" in *International Journal of Missionary Research,* July 2001.

Synan, Vinson. "The Role of Tongues as Initial Evidence." In *Conference Papers on the Theme, to the Ends of the Earth, Presented at the Twenty-third Annual Meeting of the Society for Pentecostal Studies,* 1993.

_____. "The Lasting Legacies of the Azusa Street Revival." http://enrichmentjournal.ag.org/200602/ 200602_142_legacies. cfm. Accessed Mar. 20, 2014.

The Apostolic Faith. Vol. I, No. 1, September, 1906, Los Angeles.

The Apostolic Faith. Vol I, No. 2, October 1906, Los Angeles.

Wagner, C. Peter. *Acts of the Holy Spirit.* Ventura, CA: Regal Books, 2000.

_____. "Third Wave." In *The New International Dictionary of Pentecostal and Charismatic Movements: Revised and Expanded Edition,* edited by Stanley M. Burgess and Eduard M van der Maas. Grand Rapids, MI: Zondervan, 2002.

Wimber, John. *Power Evangelism.* New York: Harper and Row Publishers, 1986.

Wright, Christopher J. H. *The Mission of God: Unlocking the Bible's Grand Narrative.* Downers Grove, IL: IVP Academic, 2006.

York, John V. *Missions in the Age of the Spirit.* Springfield, MO: Gospel Publishing House, 1999.

OTHER WORKS BY DENZIL R. MILLER

Power Ministry: How to Minister in the Spirit's Power
(2004) (Also available in French, Portuguese,
Malagasy, Kinyarwanda, and Chichewa)

*Empowered for Global Mission: A Missionary Look
at the Book of Acts* (2005)

From Azusa to Africa to the Nations (2005)
(Also available in French, Spanish, and Portuguese)

Acts: The Spirit of God in Mission (2007)
(Also available in French and Portuguese)
*In Step with the Spirit: Studies in the
Spirit-filled Walk* (2008)

*The Kingdom and the Power: The Kingdom of God:
A Pentecostal Interpretation* (2009)

*Experiencing the Spirit: A Study of the Work of
the Spirit in the Life of the Believer* (2009)

Teaching in the Spirit (2009)

*Power Encounter: Ministering in the Power and
Anointing of the Holy Spirit: Revised* (2009)
(Also available in Kiswahili)

*You Can Minister in God's Power: A Guide for
Spirit-filled Disciples* (2009)

*The Spirit of God in Mission: A Vocational
Commentary on the Book of Acts* (2011)

Proclaiming Pentecost: 100 Sermon Outlines on the Power of the Holy Spirit (2011) Associate editor with Mark Turney, editor (Also available in French, Spanish, Portuguese, and Swahili)

Globalizing Pentecostal Missions in Africa (2011) Editor, with Enson Lwesya (Also available in French)

The 1:8 Promise of Jesus: The Key to World Harvest (2012)

Power for Mission: The Africa Assemblies of God Mobilizing the Reach the Nations (2014) Editor, with Enson Lwesya

MISSIONARY TONGUES REVISITED
More than an Evidence: Recapturing Luke's Missional
Perspective on Speaking in Tongues
© 2014 Denzil R. Miller

www.ingramcontent.com/pod-product-compliance
Lightning Source LLC
Chambersburg PA
CBHW071009040426

42443CB00007B/737